Bridge in the Sky

BERLIN

FRANK DONOVAN

BRIDGE IN THE SKY

DAVID McKAY COMPANY, Inc.
NEW YORK

BRIDGE IN THE SKY

Also by FRANK DONOVAN

The Medal: The Story of the Medal of Honor

The Papers of the Founding Fathers

Riverboats of America

Wheels for a Nation

Wild Kids

The Women in Their Lives

Library of Congress Catalog Card Number: 68–29630

MANUFACTURED IN THE UNITED STATES OF AMERICA

VAN REES PRESS • NEW YORK

Author's Note

The Anglo-American airlift to supply Berlin when it was deprived of surface transportation in the summer of 1948 was a dramatic undertaking. The closing of the roads, railroads, and canals into the city by the Russians was a siege which, if successful, would have compelled the surrender of the German capital to the Communists to prevent the starvation of the populace. The airlift broke the siege, something that had never before been accomplished by airpower. When the airlift started no one believed that a city of over 2,000,000 people could be sustained exclusively by airborne supplies. It broke new ground in the logistics of airpower. It taught technical lessons that guided future air policy. But its great importance was in none of these.

The Berlin airlift was the first firm step by the Allies in the cold war that had started when the shooting war stopped, and the first clear indication to the world that the Anglo-Americans would make a staunch stand against the spread of Communism in Europe. The Russians had created their ring of Communist-controlled satellites in eastern Europe with little but token opposition by the Western powers. Their next objective was a drive to extend Communism throughout western Europe. They might

well have succeeded except for the Berlin airlift. Had
their blockade of that city been effective in driving the
Western Allies from the old German capital, it is not unreasonable to assume that they might have gained political
ascendency in all of Europe. General Lucius Clay, who
replaced General Eisenhower as the postwar Military Governor of occupied Germany, modestly described the airlift's political importance by writing:

"The success of the European Recovery Program and
the planned formation of a West German Government
led to the Soviet blockade of Berlin, a ruthless attempt to
use starvation to drive out the Western Powers, thus re-
creating in Europe the fear which favored Communist
expansion. The airlift prevented the blockade from ac-
complishing its purpose. There were risks involved in
our determination not to be driven out of the former
German capital. We understood and accepted these risks.
... To do so was essential if we were to maintain the
cause of freedom. The firm stand of the Western Powers
in undertaking the airlift not only prevented terror from
again engulfing Europe, but also convinced its free people
of our intent to hold our position until peace is assured."

F.D.

Contents

Illustrations follow page 118.

Bridge in the Sky

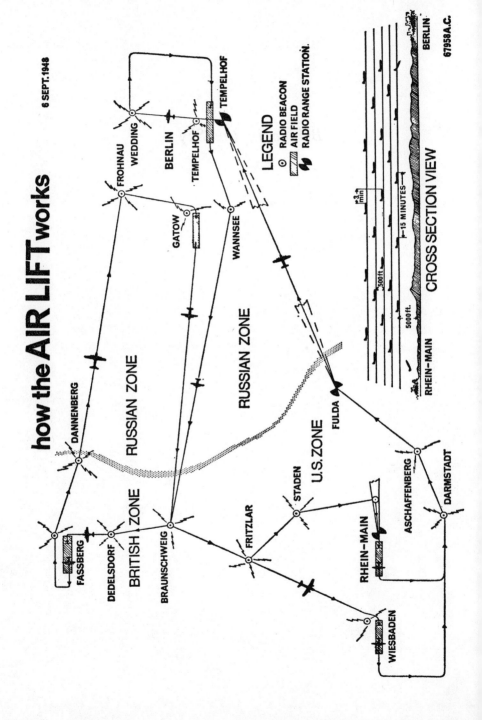

ONE

Divided City

Traditionally, American generals are not political animals. In this they differ from many of their European counterparts. Under the American system, the political relationship between countries is a matter of civilian concern and determination. In time of war, military leadership is limited to the planning of campaigns and the winning of battles to obtain decisions in the area of conflict without regard to the ultimate political effect.

Since war is an extension of international politics this concept may be a naïve one, but it has always guided American policy. In 1945 it was responsible for making the city of Berlin the focal point of a political controversy that many believed contained the seeds of World War III.

When World War II started, Berlin was the world's largest city in area and the fourth largest in population. It had been, since the early years of the twentieth century, the leading political and cultural center of central Europe, the heart of its greatest single industrial complex. It was the nerve center of Hitler's National Socialism, and by 1943, most of Europe was ruled from Berlin as a result of Nazi conquests in the early years of the war. By the time the Russians entered it, 156,000,000 pounds of English and

American bombs had reduced most of the city to acres of rubble. It no longer had much military or industrial importance. But it still had great symbolic, psychological, and political significance.

The fact that the Russians were in Berlin, rather than the Americans or the English was, in hindsight, a strategic political error for which the Allied Supreme Commander, General Dwight D. Eisenhower, has accepted the blame. At the beginning of the final phase of the war, when the Allies landed on the Normandy beaches to invade Europe on June 6, 1944, Eisenhower had named Berlin as their chief objective in a communiqué to his three army group commanders: "Clearly Berlin is the main prize and the prize in defense of which the enemy is likely to concentrate the bulk of his forces. There is no doubt whatever in my mind that we should concentrate all of our energies and resources on a rapid thrust to Berlin."

During the ensuing months the Anglo-American strategy, as directed by Eisenhower, changed; as the Russians advanced toward Berlin from the east, the Americans swept across southern Germany. In the north an Anglo-American army group of a million men, commanded by British General Sir Bernard L. Montgomery, was within striking distance of Berlin by the winter of 1944. By the early spring the American army group commanded by General Omar Bradley had reached the Elbe River, from which a fine autobahn stretched 100 miles to Berlin. Both Bradley and Montgomery wanted to advance on the city. When the American Ninth Army crossed the Elbe on April 14, 1945, its commander, General William Simpson, pleaded with his superior for permission to strike for the capital. But

Bradley had orders from *his* superior which read: "Take the necessary action to avoid offensive action in force, including the formation of new bridgeheads east of the Elbe-Mulde line . . ." General Eisenhower had changed his mind about the supreme importance of Berlin.

General Montgomery was particularly forceful in his demand that the Allies *must* take Berlin. He was convinced that if they did not the war would be lost politically, regardless of the military outcome. In reply to his appeal General Eisenhower wired: "That place has become, as far as I am concerned, nothing but a geographical location, and I have never been interested in these." General Montgomery went over Eisenhower's head and appealed to Prime Minister Winston Churchill, to whom the American commander replied, "May I point out that Berlin is no longer a particularly important objective." Churchill then sent President Roosevelt a final plea in a prophetic cable in which he said, "If the Russians take Berlin, will not their impression that they have been the overwhelming contributor to the common victory be unduly imprinted in their minds, and may not this lead them into a mood which will raise grave and formidable difficulties in the future?"

It did raise "grave and formidable difficulties," but perhaps General Eisenhower was not solely to blame in his failure to recognize that Berlin *was* a "particularly important objective" politically if not militarily. In his unwillingness to oppose the Russians in picking the plum of the campaign, he was following policy that had been established at a higher level—a policy which led to years of cold war in which the possession of Berlin became a major concern.

From the beginning of the war President Franklin Roosevelt and many of his closest advisers were firmly convinced that future world peace was absolutely dependent on cooperation between Russia, the United States, and England. Roosevelt's original concept of the postwar world was one in which these states would act as the three policemen in an otherwise disarmed world society. And he was confident that Russia would cooperate in this endeavor. True, the Russians were suspicious of their Western Allies. Historically they had cause to be. But the American President was sure that these suspicions could be allayed. Of Russia's dictator, Joseph Stalin, he said, "I think that if I give him everything I possibly can and ask nothing from him in return, *noblesse oblige,* he won't try to annex anything and will work with me for a world of democracy and peace." It took three years after the war for the fallacy of this thinking to become fully apparent; a fallacy that was finally driven home by the Berlin blockade.

Although the Russian policy was not obvious—at least to the Americans—in the spring of 1945, Churchill, Montgomery, and Eisenhower's subordinate generals were not the only ones who wanted the Western Allies to capture Berlin. In the city itself most of the estimated 2,700,000 civilians who were left—mainly women, children, and old men—prayed for liberation by the "Amis" rather than conquest by the Reds. During the final weeks of the war Berliners by the thousands listened to forbidden BBC broadcasts and eagerly plotted the progress of the Western armies on maps. Their faith in the Anglo-Americans was matched only by their fear of the Russians—a fear that approached panic as refugees from eastern Germany flocked into the city to describe the atrocities which, they said, followed Russian conquest. Those who had fled before the eastern hordes claimed that Russian propaganda was inciting the Red Army to spare no one and quoted a leaflet that was distributed among the troops telling them to, "Kill! Kill! In the German race there is nothing but evil. . . . Follow the precepts of Comrade Stalin. Stamp out the fascist beast once and for all in his lair! Use force and break the racial pride of these Germanic women. Take them as your lawful booty."

At dawn on April 16, 1945, a stupefying artillery barrage presaged the Russian crossing of the Oder and the opening of their assault on the city. On May 2, a Russian announcement stated that "after obstinate street fighting" their forces were "in complete possession of the German capital, the city of Berlin, center of German imperialism and heart of German aggression." The intervening days, and a few following days, were a period of terror for Berliners.

"Frau komm" (woman, come here) became the slogan of the marauding Red troops, many of them Mongolian and Tartar, who followed the disciplined front line forces into the city to stage an orgy of rape. Some sensationalized accounts claim that the majority of females in the city over the age of ten or twelve were raped, many of them repeatedly. A single Berlin hospital treated 230 rape victims on one particular day. In terror and desperation, hundreds of women committed suicide; in a single borough of the city, 215 suicides were recorded.

Cornelius Ryan, in his moderate, well-documented book,

The Last Battle, devotes ten pages to recounting inter-
views with observers or victims of rape. Typical was the
story of the warden in an air raid shelter who told him,
"For two days and nights wave after wave of Russians came
into my shelter plundering and raping. Women were killed
if they refused. Some were shot and killed anyway. In one
room alone, I found the bodies of six or seven women, all
lying in the position in which they had been raped, their
heads battered in."

A head nurse at the Elizabeth Hospital in Berlin told
this story of events on the morning of April 30, 1945.
"There were fearful screams from the rear wing of the
hospital. . . . All of a sudden my room was full of nurses.
We are a religious sisterhood, you know, and so most of
them were on their knees praying. Others were running
about in terror. Then the door opened. Soldiers in muddy
brown uniforms rushed in and pulled some of the nurses
out of the room. . . . I ran through the wards. Everywhere
there were Russians dragging away nurses or female patients, pulling off their clothes, pouring whisky over them,
shooting at the wall. Some Red Army men were crouching
at the window and firing at something across the street. But
then they, too, dropped their guns and took part in the
rapes. They barricaded the doors so that their comrades
would not come to take their places."

Uncontrolled looting accompanied the raping. The Russians took every personal possession of value, and much of
dubious worth. Watches, fountain pens, flashlights, and
radios were among the favorite items of loot, as was clothing, which was often stripped from victims of both sexes.
They unscrewed light bulbs and carried them off, and

ripped out lighting and toilet fixtures. Much was destroyed merely for the sake of destruction. In the International Red Cross warehouse, trigger-happy soldiers destroyed thousands of parcels containing drugs, medical supplies, and dietary foods. "They came in," said one observer, "went into the cellars, saw the huge pile of parcels and just Tommy-gunned the lot. Liquids of all sorts poured out of the shattered parcels."

The initial orgy of personal pillage was followed by several weeks of organized looting, directed by officers, which stripped the city. Machinery was removed from factories, the generators were taken from the power plants, refrigerating equipment and restaurant kitchens were ripped out, 7,000 cows on the outskirts of the city were driven away. The Russians called this "reparations," but much of the material was wrecked in removal and more was left to rust on open flatcars awaiting shipment to Russia.

As he flew into Berlin, a few months after its occupation, correspondent William Shirer wrote this description of the city as seen from the air: "The center of the capital around the Friedrichstrasse and the Leipzigerstrasse is a vast acreage of rubble. Most of the little streets I knew gone, erased off the map. The railroad stations—Potsdamer Bahnhof, Anhalter Bahnhof—gaunt shells. The Imperial Palace of the Kaisers roofless, some of its wings pulverized, and here and there the outer walls battered in. The Tiergarten, like any other battlefield from the air, pockmarked with shell holes, the old spreading trees that I had known bare stumps. And as far as you can see in all directions from a plane above the city, a great wilderness of debris, dotted with roofless, burnt-out buildings that look like little mousetraps, with the low autumn sun shining through the spaces where windows had been."

Prior to the invasion of Germany, the United States, Britain, and Russia had set up a commission to prepare plans for the occupation of the country after it was conquered. It was decided that the land should be divided into three occupation zones: the Russians in the east, the British in the northwest, and the Americans in the southwest. (French participation came later.) An Allied Control Authority, headed by the senior military commander of each nation, was established to administer and coordinate the occupation. The original members of the Control Council were Eisenhower, Montgomery for the British, and Marshal Georgi Zhukov for the Russians. Later, and throughout most of the occupation, America was represented by General Lucius D. Clay, England by General Sir Brian Robertson, Russia by Marshal Vassily D. Sokolovsky, and France by General Pierre Joseph Koenig.

Although General Clay's concern was with all of Germany rather than only Berlin, he was perhaps the most important single individual in the long cold war that determined the fate of that city. He was the man who had to make the crucial, on-the-spot decisions, and he never wavered in the basic decision that Berlin must be held at all costs. In this he could not depend on a definite U.S. policy, or an agreed U.S.-British-French policy. Such did not exist. In the absence of a determined position in relation to the Russians on the part of his allies and his Washington superiors, Clay sometimes had to make his own policy and hope for support. A *Time* correspondent quoted a Frankfort barber as saying, "I feel sorry for General Clay.

Every Russian from Marshal Sokolovsky down to the last sentry seems to know what his government's policy is and what he's supposed to do about it. With the American government I sometimes wonder whether it knows itself what it's doing."

Clay carried out his difficult job with calm assurance and a marked absence of anxiety or nervousness—although he drank cup after cup of coffee throughout the day and smoked two packs of cigarettes. His principal prewar preparation for his present post was building dams. Son of a U.S. Senator and great-grandnephew of statesman Henry ("I'd rather be right than President") Clay, he had selected the engineers upon graduation from West Point and was a captain in that corps when the war started. He had the reputation for a phenomenal memory and for being able to read about six times as fast as any other officer in the army. During the war he had been Director of Matériel for the Army Service Forces until General Eisenhower called him to Europe to break the supply bottleneck after the Normandy landing. He then worked under the Director of War Mobilization, James Byrnes, until he returned to Europe as Eisenhower's deputy. Byrnes once said of him that "He could run anything—General Motors or General Eisenhower's army." During the most critical days in Germany one observer said of Clay, "Two of the most important reasons why the West is still in Berlin and not at war with Russia are that Clay has forged a policy of firmness almost wholly on his own initiative, and that in so doing he has avoided making any fateful blunders into silly belligerence."

Berlin was within the area that had been allocated to

Russia in the preliminary plan, about a hundred miles from the border of the western zones. It was agreed that the city should be administered independently of any zone of occupation, and that it should be divided into three sectors, each to be occupied by one of the Allied powers. Under the division, Russia would get the eight eastern boroughs of the city, Britain the six northwestern boroughs, and the United States the six southwestern. Later France was included among the occupying powers, and two of the British boroughs were given to the French. To coordinate the occupation of the city, an Allied Kommandatura, with military representatives of the four powers, was established.

The American representative on the Kommandatura changed several times during the occupation, but the last and most important was Colonel (later Brigadier General) Frank Howley, who had been a reserve cavalry officer until a motorcycle accident incapacitated him for fighting duty, and he shifted to Military Government. At the beginning of the occupation he headed a unit of 150 officers, mainly reservists drawn from civilian life in which they had been lawyers, civil engineers, accountants, police officials, water sanitation engineers, transportation men, and experts in all phases of municipal management. Until the Russian purpose finally became clear, there were some who considered Howley a wild Irishman, others a stubborn Irishman, because he advocated and practiced resistance to the Russians that was not in accord with the Washington-directed policy of appeasement.

Howley's principal antagonist on the Kommandatura was Russian General Alexander Kotikov, whom Howley described as "the epitome and quintessence of the evil doctrines Moscow preaches. A big, bulky man, with flowing white hair, icy blue eyes, and a mouth like a petulant rosebud, his mind turned on and off automatically with switches operated in the Kremlin." Howley said that during the four years that he faced Kotikov, his hair turned white; but he had the satisfaction of knowing that he gave the Russian ulcers.

Howley got his first lesson on the Russian concept of cooperation before he arrived in Berlin as deputy American Commandant. When the German capital fell his unit was stationed near Hanover, waiting to move forward. Here he had found a whole village of German college girls who had succeeded in fleeing Berlin. It was a great temptation to take a flock of the *Fräuleins* along as secretaries, but the temptation was resisted. He did take a lush Horsch roadster, which his men had "liberated," as a command car and two baby wild pigs that had been captured in a boar hunt as mascots.

At daybreak on June 17, 1945, Howley set out for Berlin with the American flag flying from the fender of his Horsch. Behind him, in addition to the men of his unit, was a company of guards in armored half-tracks bristling with machine guns. In all, there were about 500 men and 120 vehicles. They proceeded without incident to the Elbe, on the other side of which they picked up a Russian officer guide in a battered German car who led them a mile down the road, where they were confronted with a roadblock. The Russian told Howley that he and the brigadier general commanding the escort were expected at headquarters.

In a rickety building beside the road, the Americans were greeted by a Russian colonel. For forty-five minutes they drank champagne and listened to a sergeant play the piano. Then, when Howley intimated that it was all very pleasant but they must be on their way, the Russian colonel asked, "How many vehicles, officers, and men do you have?"

"Roughly, five hundred officers and men and a hundred twenty vehicles."

"The agreement," said the Russian, "says thirty-seven officers, fifty vehicles, and a hundred seventy-five men."

"What agreement?" asked Howley.

"The Berlin agreement."

"We never heard of such an agreement."

"There is an agreement," said the Russian.

"Maybe somebody made an offhand estimate that we might have about that complement, but there is no agreement so far as we know. Our orders are to go to Berlin—and we're going."

"First I will have to check with headquarters."

This seemed reasonable to the Americans, who did not know that the nearest operative telephone was twenty miles away. They waited for two hours, by the end of which they were down to warm beer and sour white wine. When Howley again insisted that they were going forward, the colonel replied that he had orders from his superior to permit only the number of men and vehicles covered by the agreement to pass. Howley demanded an interview with the superior who gave the orders. After a further wait, a Russian one-star general came in, and they went through the same dreary routine: "The agreement says thirty-seven officers, fifty vehicles, and a hundred seventy-five men. That is all you can take in." Again Howley demanded to see a superior officer. This time it was a two-star general, but the dialogue was the same. Finally a three-star colonel general was summoned who brusquely told them that they had two choices: "You can cut down to the limits of the agreement and go ahead, or you can turn around and go back. That is the last word." At this point Howley sent word to General Parks, who would be the first American commandant in Berlin. Six hours later an answer came, through the Russians, that the commander of the escort was to return with the excess men and equipment, and Howley was to proceed with the number allowed by the Russians under the mythical agreement. The Soviets had won the first conflict of wills. The reduced contingent was guided forward over secondary roads to Potsdam, a suburb of Berlin, where they were kept in a compound under Russian guard until the official entry of the Allies into the capital on July 4.

For two months after the fall of Berlin the Russians had the city to themselves, and they used the time well to solidify their position. In hindsight, it became obvious that they had a clear purpose in Berlin from the first, which their allies did not recognize. Moscow regarded Germany as the key to the balance of political power in Europe; a Communist Germany would, they hoped, mean a Communist Europe. Important for this was the Communization of Berlin, for symbolic and psychological as well as economic and political reasons. Berlin was a prestige plum, the control of which would have far-reaching influence on public opinion not only in Germany but throughout Europe.

After their first few weeks of pillage and looting, the Reds set out to organize the city. The reconstituted *Magis-*

trat, the executive branch of the city government, had a non-Communist Mayor as a "front," but German Communists held most other key positions. The head of the new police force was an ex-Nazi officer who had been captured by the Russians at Stalingrad and indoctrinated as a Communist. He organized a force in which German Communists and former Nazis predominated. A centralized banking system was started under Communist control. A centralized trade union structure was set up with an executive committee on which thirty-four of the forty-five members were Communists. The two newspapers and the radio were under close Communist contol. Four political parties, including a Communist Party, were organized, presumably on an equal basis, but the Russians did everything possible to favor the Communist Party and hamper the other three. Permission was given to each party to publish a newspaper, but the Communist Party was the only one that received enough newsprint, and the papers of the other parties were so censored that the Berlin populace read or heard only Communist inspired or approved news. A rationing system was set up under which the people were divided into five categories; the highest received 2,485 calories a day, the lowest 1,248. Politicians, officials, intellectuals, and teachers, as well as those doing heavy physical labor, received the highest ration. If a German official or intellectual displeased the Soviets he might lose his preferential ration card and be condemned to slow starvation.

When the representatives of the Western Allies arrived in Berlin, they found quite an efficient city government operating amidst the rubble. The fact that it was Communist-controlled did not seem to bother them unduly. At the first meeting of the Kommandatura, the American and British representatives accepted a Soviet draft outlining operating procedures which provided that all resolutions had to be passed unanimously. At the second meeting it was agreed that all edicts and orders previously issued by the Soviet occupation forces or the city government would remain in force until changed by a resolution of the Kommandatura. Since the Russians had veto power in this body, no changes could be made in the pattern of life that they had already imposed on the city without their consent.

Of this supine acceptance of Russian domination Colonel Howley wrote: "I think it was a good indication of the policy which we were to follow in Berlin for many months, doing almost anything to win over the Russians, allay their suspicions, and convince them we were friends." Some wag described the policies of the various occupying powers by saying that the Russians were guided by greed, the British by fear, the French by concern for national honor, and the Americans by a desire to go home.

It should have been evident to anyone whose mind was not beclouded by the vision of Russians as noble allies in the cause of peace and freedom that the Soviets had no intention of cooperating to these ends. Even while they were still raping and looting, they had started a propaganda campaign to convince the populace that they had liberated the city from the Nazi tyranny while the Westerners stood by and watched. When the Anglo-Americans arrived, they found huge banners stretched across the street proclaiming: "The Red Army has saved Berlin." Portraits

of Stalin, two stories high, covered the bomb-scarred faces
of buildings, with the legend: "Stalin, the wise teacher and
protector of the working people." Over the radio and
through the press that they controlled, they hammered on
the theme that Berlin was really part of the Soviet zone of
Germany which the Russians were kindly allowing their
Western Allies to share as a symbol of solidarity. For over
two years, the Westerners disdained to use propaganda to
influence public opinion in Berlin.

Almost all of the Americans and some of the British
were completely naïve about the Russians. General Eisenhower announced that he found them very easy to get
along with. The prevalent view was that the Russians were
crude but jolly, playful fellows who drank prodigious
quantities of vodka and liked to wrestle in the living room.
On an officer level there was much socializing with the
Russians during the early part of the occupation. The
Soviets had apparently imported mountains of caviar and
lakes of vodka from their homeland, and parties came so
thick and fast that one observer said it seemed likely that
Berlin was to be pickled in vodka. It later became evident
that the Russians' insistence on "bottoms up" toasts at
these parties was a matter of policy. They were trying—
often with some success—to get the Western officers drunk
and talkative as a means of securing information.

On a G.I. level the American troops never had it so good
financially. The Russian soldiers had received two or
three years' back pay in occupation marks which the Soviets had printed by the billion. The money was no good
back in Russia; it had to be spent in Berlin. The Americans soon learned that the Russian troops had a passion

for watches, which had always been associated, in the Muscovite mind, with affluence and an exalted station in life. Enterprising G.I.s were soon sending home for dozens of cheap watches. Russian soldiers would pay up to 10,000 marks for a Mickey Mouse timepiece that cost about three dollars in the states—and the Army Finance Department would convert 10,000 marks into $1,000. A story was told of a young American lieutenant who had somehow acquired a battered old Buick sedan. One night, a junior Soviet officer appeared at his quarters with a suitcase full of money and said that he wanted to buy the car. The American was suspicious of a young officer wanting a private car—many Russian generals did not own vehicles. The Russian finally admitted that he had been sent by Marshal Zhukov to offer 200,000 marks for the car. The American sold his five-year-old Buick for $20,000.

While the conquerors played and profited among themselves, with the expectation on the part of the Westerners that all would be sweetness and light in the four-power occupation, Berliners huddled in their rubble-strewn houses, confused and apathetic after their initial disappointment at the attitude of the "Amis." For some reason they had expected that the Americans and the British would ignore the fact that the Germans were their enemies and the Russians their allies. They unreasonably anticipated that the "Amis" would protect them from the Soviets. During the weeks of unilateral Russian occupation, they had looked forward to the coming of the Westerners as children look forward to Christmas. They expected sympathy and understanding—they were shocked when the newcomers were indifferent to their woes. The

Anglo-Americans were there as a stern but fair occupation force dedicated to cooperating with the Soviets in enforcing the terms of conquest. It would take some time for the realization to dawn that the postwar enemies were the Russians, against whom the Berliners could be a staunch ally.

The initial attitude of the Allies was evidenced by an edict against fraternization. Germans might be hired as domestics or for other menial labor, but any socialization with the defeated people was declared *verboten* by the occupation authorities. This did not work out very well. Many of the Berlin girls were blond and pretty. They soon heard, for the first time in their lives, a wolf whistle as a jeep full of G.I.s slowly followed a shapely miss down the street. Then there were the children. Both British and American troops are traditionally kind and generous to children of any nation. They had, in abundance, a wonderful thing called candy, which they dispensed with open hands, so they were soon followed by queues of kids. The British and American boys were young and lonely; the girls were pretty; the kids were cute. Non-fraternization was an unenforceable edict.

On the whole, the Berliners were not concerned with the policies of the occupying forces; they were too involved in trying to stay alive in their shattered city. They huddled in broken homes behind cardboard-covered windows, two or three families to an apartment, five or six people to a room, wondering how they could trade the possessions that the Russians had missed for food. With characteristic Berlin irony, they called themselves "ruin dwellers." One correspondent likened the rooms in which they lived to something out of a surrealistic painting: "The ceiling seemed on the point of falling; only half the doors were left; in the middle of the room stood a bathtub which gathered rain water that fell through the holes in the roof; next to the tub a billiard table on which two people slept. A huge chandelier might be standing meaninglessly on the floor; it could not be used because it would have consumed too much current, but the people did not want to part with it because it was, after all, an object of value."

The principal work for Berliners was clearing rubble by hand; the "rubble women" became symbols of the defeated city. Initially, former Nazis were assigned to this as a form of punishment, but since rubble workers were entitled to the highest ration card there was soon an active competition for the jobs. Women of every class labored side-by-side, some in peasant skirts and shawls, some in high heels and silk dresses. One rubble woman described her day by saying, "I get up at six o'clock in the morning, start the stove with stolen wood, and try to swallow the ersatz coffee, and get to the ruin where I am working by seven. Some of the workers are 'party wives' as we call them—the wives of Nazis who at first were made to work on the ruins but have stayed at it even though they don't have to anymore. Then there are the 'gold diggers,' pretty young things who get intimate with the director of operations and spend their time sitting in the warm office. And there are very old women who go to the employment offices and plead that they'll starve to death unless they are given some job. They work themselves so frightfully hard every day that we expect them to fall down dead. I have to clean a thousand bricks a day ... the first day I did barely four hundred, but after three weeks I reached twelve hundred. I am paid about twenty-eight marks a week."

Because of the inflation due to the Russian-printed currency, the economy of Berlin was based on cigarettes. For a time, cigarettes would buy anything on the black market —but money would not buy cigarettes, legally. No tobacco was sold in Berlin after May 2. A single cigarette in the summer of 1945 had a black-market money value of fifteen to twenty marks—$1.50 to $2.00 at the arbitrary rate of exchange established by the American Army Finance Department. A pack of American cigarettes had an established black-market rate of $30 but its actual purchasing power was two or three times that, so that a true value of a pack of Chesterfields was $75 to $90. Butt collecting became the principal spare time occupation of most Berliners. An American who paused on the street while smoking a cigarette was soon the center of a circle of children and whiskered old men, waiting to dive for the butt when he dropped it.

The economic power of the cigarette is illustrated by the story of the first motion picture made in the western sector of Berlin. After the Russians set up a well-financed movie-making operation in their zone, for propaganda purposes, the British gave an enterprising German a license to make a picture in the old UFA studio near Tempelhof airport. Sets were standing from a picture that had been in production when the city fell. The producer easily collected a cast and crew, but the crew was so weak from hunger that they could not do a full day's work. Also, the black-market price of film was prohibitive. Both problems were solved through some American officers who had

befriended the pretty actresses. They were generous with
cartons of cigarettes, with which film and black-market ingredients for a nourishing mid-day stew were obtained.
The picture, which was a smashing success when it was
released in Berlin, was financed by Camels, Chesterfields,
and Lucky Strikes.

The most important factor in the life of the average
Berliner during the occupation was the black market. Anything could be purchased on the black market, with cigarettes as the preferred currency. The market started in the
neighborhood of the Brandenburg Gate at the junction of
the eastern and western zones, but soon spread to the Tiergarten and elsewhere throughout the city. It opened at
about ten in the morning, when children appeared to bar-
ter cigarettes that they had begged from G.I.s. They were
followed by peasants with farm produce and professional
traders with every conceivable type of portable consumer
goods. Although the occupying authorities tried to sup-
press the black market in a half-hearted way, the occupying forces were its best customers. And it was hard to get
convictions against big-time black-market operators; like
other Berliners, judges and prosecutors were dependent on
its continued operation. There were frequent raids by the
M.P.s of all nations and the Berlin police, but buyers and
sellers always seemed to know when the raids were imminent and drifted out of the area to assemble some place
else. One correspondent reported that he bought a pound
of butter for $120 in cigarettes, a pound of coffee for $60,
a bottle of popskull schnapps for $200, and a pair of silk
stockings for $25.

Companion to the black market was the swap market

in which Germans traded their remaining personal possessions and household goods through signs posted at central locations or ads in the papers. Every conceivable kind of swap was proposed. One reporter noted proposals to swap X-ray film for dental treatment; two men's suits, a winter coat, and two pairs of shoes for a bedroom and kitchen; a hairdrier for men's trousers; and an alarm clock for bed linen. Another correspondent reported offers on the swapboard near press headquarters to trade a pair of men's heavy shoes for tobacco; an electric icebox for a Leica camera; food or cigarettes for an English dictionary or a cigarette lighter in good condition; a rabbit hutch and a garden hose for a stud rabbit; twenty Macedonian cigarettes for a pound of sugar; twenty-five cigarettes for a bottle of German brandy; tobacco for Russian lessons— and one from a female with an eye on a singing career who sought to trade a beautiful old china cabinet for an evening dress, evening shoes, and some operatic music scored for a soprano.

In addition to their other troubles, Berliners had to contend with a wave of lawlessness during the early period of the occupation. In a city that saw but forty murders in an entire prewar year, there were 535 violent civilian deaths in the first eleven months of the occupation. An unarmed, poorly equipped police force accounted for some of this. In the American zone, with a population of almost a million, the police had only two dozen old cars, a handful of battered motorcycles, twenty-four bicycles, six tricycles, and no communications equipment. There were fewer than five thousand homes with telephones in all of Berlin, and to summon police aid it might be necessary to run thirty or forty blocks. Robbery was the cause of most crimes of violence; if a man is hungry enough, violence becomes a minor matter in his search for food or the wherewithal to buy it. Much of the crime was traceable to hundreds of Red Army deserters who were prowling the city in civilian clothes, without papers or ration cards, who had to kill to live.

An impression of the mental state of Berliners and the incredible things that were happening in the city may be gained from the story of the blind man that almost every correspondent cabled home in late 1945. A girl was walking along the Knesebeckstrasse when a blind man bumped into her (for some reason, in most of the reports it was a pretty girl). The blind man had a letter in his hand. The girl apologized for getting in his way and asked if she could help him. As a matter of fact, she could. "I have to deliver this letter," he said, "but I have walked miles today and I am very tired. Could you deliver it for me?" The girl looked at the address. It was several blocks away but not too far out of her path, so she agreed to deliver it. However, she first stopped in a store a short distance away, and when she came out she saw the same blind man giving a letter to another girl. Her suspicions aroused, she went to the police. When they visited the apartment to which the letter was addressed, they found two men and a woman and a quantity of meat—which turned out to be human flesh. The letter contained a single sentence:"This may be the last one I am sending you today."

The story was pure myth, but every Berliner believed it, and correspondents were told by their informants that they knew the girl to whom it had happened. It was so uni-

versally believed because it was something that might well
have happened in the bizarre condition of occupied Berlin.

The spirit of brotherly love was sorely tried from the
very beginning at meetings of the Kommandatura. The
Russians were so exasperating that the Western representatives had difficulty adhering to the policy of appeasement that had been handed down from on high. Using the
tactic by which they would later ham-string the Security
Council of the United Nations, the Soviets vetoed any proposed action that was not to their advantage or of which
they were suspicious—and they were suspicious of almost
anything proposed by their allies. They even vetoed an
American proposal for the control of potato bugs, presumably on the grounds that, since anything *they* did had a
political motivation, there must be some political significance to this American plan.

The only agreements that could be reached were more
or less on Russian terms, and frequently involved some
farcical face-saving compromises. For instance, shortly after
the Americans occupied their sector, they posted announcements beside the decrees that had been put up by the
Russians. Red troops, roaming the sector, promptly tore
down the American announcements. When the Americans
complained at the Kommandatura, the Russians replied
that the American announcements, posted beside those of
the Soviets, "created confusion." Finally, the Americans
agreed not to post any more announcements in return for
a Russian agreement not to tear any more down.

Some aspects of the Russian harassment of their allies
on the Kommandatura were amusing—except to the par-
ticipants. One such instance was the Russian insistence on

the time of day that meetings should start. Generally, Americans get up early, eat a hearty breakfast, go to work not later than nine o'clock, and are ready for lunch about twelve. The British start a little later and prefer a one o'clock lunch. The Russians like to work at night and sleep in the morning, eating breakfast around eleven and lunch late in the afternoon. Based on these habits, the Russians insisted on starting lengthy meetings at noon so that their allies got no lunch. Colonel Howley said, facetiously, that they were so hungry by four o'clock that they would agree to anything.

The first major problem of the joint occupation of Berlin was the Russian refusal to supply food for the western sections of the city. This was a matter that had never been discussed because it was assumed that food for Berlin would come from where it had always come from— the provinces of Brandenburg and Pomerania to the east of the city, in the Russian sector of Germany. Further, before the German surrender, the Americans had occupied the rich agricultural provinces of Thuringia and Saxony, to the south, which they had turned over to the Soviets, for inclusion in the Russian zone, at the time of the partition of Berlin. The Russians controlled most of the food-producing areas of Germany; West Germany, scarcely able to feed itself, could not possibly feed Berlin. Washington finally agreed to take responsibility for the food supply of West Berlin, since Britain had no surplus. The English, in turn, supplied coal for the western zones from the German Ruhr, which was within their sector of occupation.

This food and fuel would come into Berlin from the

western zones of Germany by way of one rail line, the fine autobahn for cars and trucks, and a network of canals. However, the occupation plans established by the Allied Control Authority made no *formal* provision for access to the city from the western zones—the use of access routes by the Westerners was, in effect, an informal gentlemen's agreement. There had been no specific discussion of the matter; there was no written understanding. General Clay later took the blame for this, but at the time, when "getting along with the Russians" was top policy, he felt that insistence on access routes under Anglo-American control would have been construed by the Russians as an act of bad faith. Since these access routes ran through Russian-controlled territory, they were supervised and maintained by the Russians.

Late in 1945, a formal agreement was reached for three twenty-mile-wide air corridors connecting Berlin with Hanover, Hamburg, and Frankfurt in the western zone. These were supervised by a four-power Air Safety Control. Russian air safety practices were so primitive that they were willing to sign this agreement in order to get Anglo-American "know-how" to control all air traffic in Berlin.

So things stood until the fall of 1946, with the Anglo-Americans leaning over backwards in their effort to be cooperative while the Soviets stubbornly demanded their own terms. The first break in the pattern came not from the Western Allies, but from the Berliners themselves.

Despite Russian propaganda and the special privileges accorded its members, the Communist Party in Berlin had not attracted membership. The strongest of the four political parties in the city was the labor-oriented Social

Democrat Party, which had existed before the war. In the summer of 1946, the Russians proposed a merger of the Communist Party and the Social Democrats and coerced the leadership of the latter party into agreeing to the formation of a new party to be called the Socialist Unity Party—which would be Communist-controlled. The name suggested that the Soviets favored a united Germany and their propaganda stressed this while accusing the "American imperialists" of seeking to divide the country. They were sure that "unity" was a magic word that would cause the people to flock to the standard of the new party.

What the Russians did not understand was that Berliners were a rather special breed of Germans, somewhat cynical, sophisticated, and apt to regard politics and politicians with a jaundiced eye. Hitler's National Socialism had much less support in Berlin than in any other part of Germany—Berliners had voted against Hitler so long as free elections were allowed in Germany. They were now more skeptical of Communism than they had been of National Socialism—and they had not forgotten *"Frau komm."* The rank and file of the Social Democrats repudiated their leaders and demanded a referendum on the merger with the Communist Party. The result was a smashing defeat for the Communists when 82 percent of the Social Democrats in the western sectors of Berlin voted against amalgamation. In the eastern section of the city the Russians closed the polls when they saw the trend of the voting and announced that the merger had been passed.

It was a small election—not more than 25,000 voted in the city—but it was the first concrete step in opposition to Russian domination and aggression. This handful of

Berliners had risen from political apathy and gone on record that they would defy the Communists, with or without the support of the Western occupation powers.

Hard on the heels of this first defeat for the Russians came approval by the Allied Control Council for a free election of a Berlin government to replace the one that had been appointed by the Soviets when the city was first occupied—a proposal which Kotikov's veto in the Kommandatura had stymied for months. When the superior occupation authority overruled the Kommandatura, the Russians inaugurated a frantic preelection campaign to influence Berliners by bribery, threats, and propaganda. The center of the city looked like Moscow on May Day, with mammoth posters proclaiming: "The Soviet Union is the friend of the German working people," "Turn back the warmongers," "New Germany marches to peace with our Soviet brothers." The free parties were refused as much as a minute of time on Berlin's only, Soviet-controlled, radio station. Socialist Unity broadcasts and blaring sound trucks deafened the city. Democratic candidates who entered the Russian sector of the city put their lives in danger from Red "goon-squads" when they crossed over. Several were beaten, and one disappeared—his body was later found floating in a lake.

On another front, the Soviets permitted fresh fruits and vegetables to flow into the western sectors—saying, by inference, "Vote Social Unity and you'll eat better." They passed out cigarettes to workers, shoes to children, and coal briquets stamped with the emblem of their party. And if the carrot did not work, they had the whip. They curtailed the flow of electric power from East to West

Berlin, where they had previously stripped the biggest generating plant. They started a rumor that the Westerners would depart from the city after the elections, leaving those who had voted against Social Unity at the mercy of the Communists.

None of this seemed to influence the Berliners. On October 20, 1946, 92 percent of those eligible to vote turned out to vote down the Communists. The Social Democrats polled 48.7 percent of the vote. The two smaller parties, the Christian Democrats and the Liberal Democrats, received 22.2 percent and 9.3 percent of the vote respectively. The Social Unity Party got only 19.2 percent. Even in the Russian sector of the city, the Communist-controlled party polled only 21 percent of the vote—a smaller share than the Communist Party had drawn in Berlin before Hitler. The raping and looting practiced by the Russian army had caused a reaction against all things Communist, in the minds of the Berliners.

The October elections convinced the Russians that they could never control Berlin with the consent of its people. The city could become a symbol for the Communists in western Europe only as a result of force and coercion. Possession of this symbol was, in their minds, an essential step in the spread of Communism throughout Germany, and, they hoped, in France and Italy. Most political observers believed that if Berlin fell to the Russians, Communism could not be stopped short of the Pyrenees. Before they could control the city, the Soviets would have to force the Western Allies out. To this end, they intensified their reign of terror in Berlin after the elections.

The Russians now became more vehement in their

assertions that Berlin was part of the Soviet zone of Germany. On the Allied Control Council, Marshal Sokolovsky accused the Anglo-Americans of using "their position to prejudice their right to remain in Berlin." On the political front, the Russians sought to discredit the newly elected city Assembly by refusing, in the Kommandatura, to approve the Lord Mayor whom the Assembly had selected. The City Hall was in the Soviet Zone and communications addressed to the Lord Mayor were returned by the Russians with the statement that there was no such individual.

The Russians played up the rumor that the Western Allies were about to leave Berlin to the point where even *The New York Times* gave it credence, and the more timid among Western military government personnel began to think that it might be advisable to depart gracefully before being summarily ejected. As part of the war of nerves, high Red Army officers cruised the better residential sections of the western zones, presumably selecting preferred billets that they would take after the Allies had left.

There was no concrete pattern to the Russian terror tactics and harassment. Relatively minor incidents were interspersed with wholesale kidnappings, in the western sectors, by the MVD. Hundreds of active anti-Communists disappeared into the night, including four judges whose decisions displeased the Soviets. A common pattern for a kidnapping was for a car to whisk down a street in one of the western sectors and come to a screaming halt as men in civilian clothes jumped out and grabbed a victim. The car then raced into the Russian sector and the subject was seen no more. Complaints to Kotikov were met by the bland statement that he knew nothing about it but would "investigate."

The Russians tried to push as far as they could without arousing active Anglo-American opposition, but when they met firm resistance they usually backed down. Typical was an incident at the German Railway Administration Building. This was in the American sector but, since the Russians controlled the operation of the railroads, it was staffed by Russian supervisory personnel. One night armed Russian troops appeared and took up positions around the building. Colonel Howley immediately sent American troops to surround them. When the Americans deployed and set up machine guns, the Russians withdrew within the building. So things stood until about one A.M., when Howley received a telephone call from Kotikov.

"How is Mrs. Howley?" said the Russian sweetly.

Immediately suspicious at the Russian's excessive politeness, Howley answered, "Fine."

"By the way," continued Kotikov, "an awkward situation has developed in our building."

"Your building?"

"Well, the German Railway Administration Building. I thought you ought to know that American soldiers are down there and that one of them has just stuck a Tommy gun in General Petrov's stomach."

"Well," said Howley, "I will certainly investigate the matter and call you in the morning."

"Oh, no," said the Russian. "There may be shooting."

"Our soldiers are well disciplined," replied Howley, curtly, "I hope yours are, too." He hung up. At dawn the Russians filed out of the building, climbed into their trucks, and went away. There was no further attempt to place armed Russian guards in the American sector.

There were many instances of individual armed Russians running amok in the western sector. The unarmed Berlin police were forbidden to take action against members of the armed forces of any of the occupying powers. They were given cards with the words "rape," "assault," "murder," "robbery," and "burglary" printed in French and English. When they detected a Russian soldier committing one of these acts, they sought out the nearest M.P.s of the sector in which it was happening and exhibited the proper card. When the M.P.s arrived, the Russians sometimes brandished guns, and several of the gun wielders were shot by American M.P.s. The British used a different system. They disarmed the culprit, beat him unmercifully, knocking out a few teeth, and threw him back in the Russian zone. Their tactics seemed to be more effective. A sidelight of this is that the Russians, although they brandished guns freely, never used them. They were quick to *threaten* the use of force, but hesitant about using it, an attitude which should have had more significance to policy-makers on the Western side who were influenced by fear of war with Russia.

Measures that ultimately led to the complete strangulation of traffic between Berlin and West Germany started in 1948 when, on January 24, a British military train was stopped and two cars containing German passengers were detached. This began a succession of incidents, each more provoking than the last. The Soviets demanded the right to board trains and check the identity of individual passengers. When this was refused, trains were shunted

onto sidings for countless hours. Freight trains were held
on the excuse that their cargoes had to be examined, piece
by piece, for smuggled items. Motor traffic on the autobahn
was repeatedly halted on the grounds that the road had to
be repaired. Finally, the Soviets refused to pass any military
passenger train across the West German border en route
to Berlin unless baggage and passengers were checked and
approved by the Russians. The Americans promptly dispatched a test train with armed guards to determine
whether the Russians would attempt to use force. The
train was electrically switched onto a siding, where it sat
for some time before it ignominiously retreated.

The Soviets seemed to be completely capricious in their
interference with traffic. One correspondent remarked
that they did it "with the galling casualness of kids playing jackknife in their own back yard, which is how they
regard Berlin." One time they closed an American-built
bridge over the Elbe "for repairs." This forced cars to
detour over dirt roads and cross on a small ferry. Then
the Soviets opened the bridge again. No repairs were in
evidence. For two or three successive days they might turn
back all cars coming from Berlin at the exit checkpoint
at Helmstedt, on the border of the English zone, claiming
that the drivers did not have a proper pass. As cars were
not allowed to remain in the Soviet zone overnight, this
meant returning the hundred-odd kilometers to Berlin to
try again tomorrow. The next day, the same officer might
smilingly wave all cars through.

By the spring of 1948, it should have been apparent that
matters in Berlin were approaching a showdown, although
few preparations were made to counter a Soviet move to

isolate the city. True, in April there was a "baby airlift" which brought necessities to Allied occupation personnel when General Clay suspended military train service rather than submit to Soviet inspection. When Russia stopped shipments of fresh milk into the western zones of the city, condensed and powdered milk were stockpiled in the American zone, and baby's formulas based on these substitutes were published in the newspapers. Before all land communications were cut off, the Western Allies had succeeded in stockpiling about thirty-six days of minimum food supplies in the city and a forty-five-day supply of coal.

When Russia walked out of the Allied Control Authority on March 20, 1948, it became obvious to the most die-hard advocate of getting along with the Reds that the four-party administration of Germany had collapsed. If Germany was to be united it would have to be on Russian terms. The alternative, toward which both the British and Americans were trending, was a division of the country into a democratic West Germany and a Communist East Germany. This left Berlin isolated 100 miles within the Communist country.

There was much difference of opinion in Washington and London as to whether Berlin could be held in such a situation—and some question as to whether the attempt should be made. The Russians were rattling the saber vigorously. There were many who feared that outright defiance of Russia in Berlin might lead to war—and wondered whether the city was worth the risk. Surely, said the timid souls, at least American dependents should be removed from Berlin. Fortunately, General Clay was firmly convinced that Russia would not fight for Berlin. When queried by the War Department on the advisability of evacuating American families he replied, "Withdrawal of dependents from Berlin would create hysteria accompanied by a rush of Germans to Communism for safety. This condition would spread in Europe and would increase Communist political strength everywhere.... Our women and children can take it, and they appreciate import. There are few here who have any thought of leaving unless required to do so."

General Clay did not believe that the Russians would try to blockade Berlin—to force the hand of the Westerners by denying Berliners the necessities of life. The idea of starving or freezing the bulk of the population of a major city—most of them women and children—for a political advantage was so barbaric as to be unbelievable. Also, Clay said, "I doubted if the Russians would be so foolish as to make a move which would alienate the German population completely." If they did succeed in cutting off the food supply, the allies might be forced to withdraw to prevent starvation of the populace. But, he added, "when Berlin falls, western Germany will be next. If we mean ... to hold Europe against Communism we must not budge. We can take humiliation and pressure, short of war, in Berlin without losing face. If we withdraw, our position in Europe is threatened. If America does not understand this now, does not know that the issue is cast, then it never will, and Communism will run rampant. I believe that the future of democracy requires us to stay.... This is not an heroic pose because there will be nothing heroic in having to take humiliation without retaliation."

The Soviets, by this time, were fully committed to forcing the Western Allies out of Berlin. An East German journalist, who later defected to the West, recalled a conversation with Colonel Tulpanov, Russian propaganda chief, about two months before the blockade became complete. He asked the Russian, "I should like to have directives from you on our approach in combating the constant slanders in the Western press that the Soviet authorities intend to throttle Berlin. How do you think we should handle these libelous assertions?"

Tulpanov replied, "In West Berlin an operation center of Western imperialists has been established under the leaderships of Clay and Howley. They are . . . ruthlessly exploiting West Berlin. . . . We permitted them to come to Berlin in order that they might cooperate with us in building a peaceful, progressive, demilitarized, and democratic Germany. But for months you have seen Clay sabotaging all such efforts. . . . The Soviet Union considers Berlin the capital of a united Germany. The imperialists, on the other hand, have come here to split Germany. The German people need not stand for that. And, I tell you, the Americans will get out of this city!"

On June 20, 1948, the Russians walked out of the Kommandatura. There was no longer a semblance of four-power unity. Three days later the teletypes of the Soviet-sponsored news agency in the offices of the newspapers of West Berlin typed out: "Berlin, June 23. . . . Transport Division of the Soviet Military Administration is compelled to halt all passenger and freight traffic to and from Berlin tomorrow at 0600 hours because of technical difficulties. . . . It is impossible to reroute traffic in the interests of maintaining rail service, since such measures would unfavorably affect the entire railroad traffic in the Soviet Occupation Zone." Later, a second message proclaimed: "Water traffic will be suspended. Coal shipments from the Soviet Zone are halted. The Soviet authorities have also ordered the central switching stations to stop the supply of electric power from the Soviet Zone and the Soviet Sector to the Western Sector. Shortage of coal to operate the plants is the reason."

The autobahn was also closed to vehicular traffic due to "technical difficulties," the excuse that the Russians blandly advanced for what General Clay described as "one of the most ruthless efforts in modern times to use mass starvation for political coercion."

TWO

The Flight of the Gooney Birds

One evening late in June, 1948, General Lucius Clay and Lieutenant General Albert Wedemeyer sat long over dinner. As chief of the Planning and Operations Division of the U.S. General Staff, Wedemeyer had nothing to do, directly, with affairs in Germany or Berlin. He was there by chance, but it was a fortunate chance, for Wedemeyer was one of the few non-airmen in the world who appreciated the potentialities of air transport. Until the end of the war in the Pacific, he had commanded United States Forces in China where his men, and the Chinese troops, had for three years been supplied principally by planes flying over the Hump of the Himalayas from India.

The dinner table conversation naturally centered on the most pressing immediate problem: the Berlin blockade. Not for a moment did General Clay consider getting out of the besieged city. But the Westerners could not stay in it without supplies. Clay's first thought was to send an armed convoy down the autobahn to fight its way into the city if necessary. He was convinced that fighting would not be necessary; the Russians would not risk all-out war to support the position they had taken in Berlin. The powers in the Pentagon did not share his conviction. Reliance on the Russians as peace-loving allies had been replaced by unreasonable fear of Russian military might. Although throughout the cold war, the Soviets had never resorted to force, and had several times backed away from situations which might have led to fighting, the prevailing opinion in Washington was that the Soviets might employ their vastly superior forces in Europe if they were challenged in Berlin. Clay was told that he could send his tanks and armored cars down the autobahn—but they were not to shoot. If challenged they were to return. Such a restriction would make the activity a meaningless gesture and no convoy was sent.

General Wedemeyer had another idea. "Why not," he asked Clay, "consider supplying the city by air? There is no question of your being able to support your position in Berlin by air if enough airplanes are made available."

Airlifting supplies to a besieged force was not a new concept. As long ago as 1916, cloth covered, open-cockpit planes of the Royal Flying Corps had endeavored to air supply 9,000 British troops surrounded by the Turks at Kut, near Baghdad. They swooped low over the town to drop 200-pound packages—their maximum load. The supplies thus delivered were not sufficient to maintain the defenders. In World War II the Russians made an almost equally primitive—and equally unsuccessful—effort to relieve besieged Leningrad by air. Later a German effort to air supply their forces surrounded at Stalingrad also failed, although the requirements were only 300 tons a day.

The only successful air lift had been over the Hump, in the China-Burma-India theater, which had flown food, oil, ammunition, medical supplies, mules, and machinery to

China to supply 60,000 Americans and partially serve 19 Chinese Armies. The Hump operation had lasted for three years and, in its best month, had flown 72,000 tons over the mountains. But the logistics of the Hump airlift were very different from those that would apply in Berlin. In the former, supplies had been flown from thirteen bases in the Assam Valley, Bengal Valley, and Calcutta to nine alternative air fields in Ghengtu and Kunming. In bad weather there was a wide choice of landing fields and an unlimited choice of routes, and the operation could be interrupted for several days if necessary. Contrarily, an airlift to Berlin would have to operate every day, or almost every day, in all kinds of weather, and was limited to three twenty-mile-wide corridors and two landing fields at the Berlin end. And 72,000 tons a months was little more than half the *minimum* needed to keep Berlin alive. Wede-meyer's suggestion might apply to air supplying the oc-cupation forces, but not to the total population for any length of time.

On the morning of June 24, General Clay called General Curtis LeMay, chief of USAFE (U.S. Air Forces in Europe) to ask him if his planes could perform what he considered "a very big operation." Could they supply the needs of the American occupation forces in Berlin by lifting 500 or 700 tons a day from the Rein-Main air base near Frankfort to Templehof airfield in the beleaguered city? "It would not be for long," said Clay, "perhaps three or four weeks." The American general still thought that this blockade was merely the latest of many Russian harassing tactics. He could not believe that the Soviets would deliberately con-demn over 2,000,000 people to starvation in order to further their political aims. LeMay replied that USAFE could deliver whatever the Military Governor required. When he named Brigadier General Joseph Smith to supervise the operation, he specified that the assignment was for forty-five days. There was no thought then, even in the minds of the airmen, of supplying the entire population of Berlin with food, to say nothing of the fuel that would be required when winter set in. Nor was there a planned approach to using the airplane as a diplomatic weapon to break the Russian stranglehold and to stem the spread of Communism. Initially, the airlift was a measure to gain time to negotiate in Germany and Moscow.

The operation needed a name and, with characteristic concern for the dramatic, USAFE public relations proposed to call it "Operation Lifeline." This seemed a little too pretentious for what was then contemplated and, since food was the principal initial cargo, the more prosaic title "Operation Vittles" was adopted. It was not long before some wag dubbed the airlift "LeMay Coal and Feed Company—round-the-clock service—delivery guaranteed."

USAFE was, at the time, merely an occupation air force. The 12,000 American planes that had darkened the skies over Europe three years previously had long since flown home. Most were lined up in endless rows in Arizona waiting to be junked. LeMay had been left with a handful of fighters and bombers and, for transports, two troop carrier groups of C-47s, affectionately known as Gooney Birds.

The Gooney Bird was a twin-engine passenger plane commercially known as the DC-3. Designed in 1934, it had quickly become the mainstay of the commercial airlines. It had a cruising speed of 170 miles an hour and a carrying capacity, for a short haul, of about three tons. It was not designed as a freighter. In fact, the Air Force, at that time, did not own any planes specifically designed to carry cargo, other than a few prototypes of future models. Most of the Gooney Birds in Europe were weary war veterans, many painted with the three horizontal stripes that identified them as craft used in the Normandy invasion six years before. A few others had seen better days flying the Hump in the China-Burma-India theater. By combing the continent to take staff planes away from generals and diplomats, thirty-odd additional Gooney Birds were added to the two troop carrier wings to provide a total of 110 aircraft, each capable of carrying three tons, to start the airlift. On the first day, June 25, thirty-two flights landed eighty tons in Berlin, mostly milk for children, flour, and medicine.

Meanwhile, the British had not been idle. From the American press of the time, one would get the impression that the airlift was an all-American operation, made possible by Yankee skill, daring, and ingenuity. Actually, the British carried between a quarter and a third of the total tonnage throughout the entire operation. They called their DC-3s Dakotas and their airlift, "Operation Plane Fare." At first, the two airlifts were independent operations, the British flying from their base at Fassberg to Gatow airport in the British zone of Berlin. Ultimately, the two lifts were combined into a single operation, with American planes flying from British bases. The French, whose resources in aircraft numbered six battered Junkers and one Dakota, were dependent on their allies for supplies.

The geography of the occupation zones added to the

complexities of the airlift. The two American air bases, Weisbaden and Rein-Main, were close together at the western end of the southernmost corridor, respectively 281 and 267 miles from Berlin. The British had seven bases adjacent to the center and northernmost corridors. Their principal fields were at Fassberg and Celle, each about 150 miles from Berlin. It was immediately recognized that a large volume of two-way traffic in any corridor would not be feasible from a safety standpoint, so the British used the northern corridor to fly into the city, the Americans the southern corridor, and both flew out in the center corridor. This considerably increased the round-trip distance, particularly for the Americans because they had a dog leg to fly on the return trip. The round trip from Rein-Main was 603 miles, from Fassberg, 320 miles.

The principal American departure base, Rein-Main, was called "the aerial gateway to Europe," and when the airlift started it was used by ten commercial airlines and was the European terminal for MATS (Military Air Transport Service). Prior to World War II, its 2,000 acres had been the home port for the German lighter-than-air service. It was from Rein-Main that the zeppelin *Hindenburg* had departed on her ill-fated voyage that ended in flames over Lakehurst, N.J. The *Luftwaffe* had converted the dirigible station into a fighter base, which became a prime target for Allied bombs. What was left of the base when the occupation armies neared was completely destroyed by German demolition squads before the surrender. By 1948, American Army engineers had restored the facility so that it was adequate for its normal use, but not for the additional capacity required by the airlift.

Templehof, the airfield in the American sector of Berlin, was far less adequate than Rein-Main. In fact, it would have been hard to find an airport in any major city in the world that was less suited to the needs of the airlift than Templehof. Back in the late 1920s and early 1930s, after Lindbergh's flight made America air-minded, Templehof was regularly visited by delegations from American cities who came to inspect it as a model of an advanced municipal airport. It had one sodded runway. What was advanced in the late 1920s was obsolete in the late 1940s; and in 1945 Templehof still had one sodded runway. The Germans had used it during the war only as a base for light fighter planes to defend the city. The Nazis had built a tremendous administration building, with five stories above ground and seven below, which had, at one time, housed a large subterranean hospital and a complete assembly plant making Messerschmidt planes. Before the Americans arrived, the Russians had dynamited the building's pumps and ventilating system, making most of the underground installation inaccessible. In any event, a gigantic administration building was not what the airlift needed in Berlin, although it could have been put to good use in Rein-Main. By 1948, American engineers had "improved" the airport to the extent of building another runway—a base of rubble topped with metal landing strips. Planes landed on the metal and took off on the sod.

Templehof was located in downtown Berlin, a location which made it handy for commercial travelers, but dangerous as a landing site in bad weather. Except for a graveyard on one side, it was closely surrounded by apartment buildings. In war-torn Berlin, starved for housing, nothing could be done about removing them to make it easier to run an airlift. But it seemed reasonable that something could be done about one particular flying hazard; the 400-foot chimney of a brewery that towered almost on the edge of the landing field. Immediately after the airlift started, steps were taken through Berlin government channels to get rid of the smokestack. These led to the fiercely determined, stubborn, and tenacious brewer who owned the chimney. The smokestack had been there before the airport was laid out in 1922. His beer, claimed the brewmaster, was essential to Germany's economic welfare, and his smokestack was an aesthetic asset in the bomb-gutted metropolis. He had stood firm against the Nazis and risked a concentration camp when they tried to make him take down the pride of his brewery, and he would stand with equal firmness against the Americans. Throughout the airlift, planes continued to fly around the smokestack.

In the beginning, the airlift was what its ultimate commander, General William H. Tunner, called a "cowboy operation." Things had been rather deadly-dull for fliers of the occupation air force. Now they responded to the challenge with a revival of the war-time spirit of derring-do. This "can-do" attitude was what was needed to get the operation off the ground, literally and figuratively. Without regard for other consequences, USAFE, from General LeMay down to the newest Pfc. in the ground crew, pitched in to "get the serum to Nome."

Although most of the initial planes were those of two-troop carrier squadrons, USAFE personnel, on the whole, were fighting fly-boys who had little experience using planes for transport rather than combat. General LeMay had made an outstanding reputation during the war through pioneering experiments that improved the effectiveness of long-range bombing operations. Commanding B-17s in Europe, he found that pilots usually tried to dodge antiaircraft fire, with the result that bombing aims were spoiled. He ordered that, regardless of flak, the last few minutes of the run must be on a straight course to the target and piloted the lead plane of the first squadron himself to show how it was done. Later, commanding B-29s in the Pacific, he initiated the tactic of coming in very low over Japanese cities to minimize the effect of antiaircraft fire. He had also directed the dropping of the atomic bombs on Hiroshima and Nagasaki. None of this had much relation to delivering supplies to a besieged city.

On the administrative level, personnel were equally inexperienced in the type of flying called for by an airlift. On the first day of operation General Smith called his staff together and assigned each man a job, somewhat in the manner of a captain of a sandlot baseball team saying, "you pitch, you catch, you play short-stop." Major Edward Willerford later recalled that when he was assigned to be the air cargo officer he did not know the carrying capacity of a C-47. The same was true of operations officers and ground-control officers. Their training for combat flying did not embrace this type of routine delivery operation.

The pilots of the 60th and 61st Troop Carrier Wings, the first fliers on the scene, were transport men; but they were used to flying troops and sometimes matériel on special missions, not to running a shuttle service. The stereotype pilot was still the war-time, crushed-hat fly-boy immortalized in Steve Canyon. None fancied himself as an aerial truck driver. The attitude of the fliers was evident from a humorous argument as to whether, in this type of work, they should be called pilots or drivers. One flier, looking around at the conditions in which they were living, settled the discussion by saying, "Just call us peasants, boys—just peasants." Still, somehow, the job got under way.

The principal difficulty in the first few weeks was to find enough pilots and aircrews. The normal complements of the troop carrier wings were not sufficient to keep the planes in the air around the clock. Men with wings were pulled from desks in non-flying departments—maintenance, public relations, photographic, etc.—and returned to the air to give the active fliers a minimum of rest. Still, the fliers worked incredible hours. Scores of those who started flying the airlift on its first day crowded 160 flying hours into the next four weeks. Captain Hugo Krenek of the 60th Troop Carrier Wing later recalled: "Things were pretty confused. After awhile they seemed less confused and just plain rugged. Then a little later, things weren't rugged anymore; instead, we all just seemed to be exhausted. I flew 158 hours the first month, and 68 percent of the flights were on instruments. Pretty soon I said to myself, 'Boy, you aren't grouchy. You're just about on the verge of being done in.'"

The flight surgeon of the 60th, Lieutenant Robert Miller, reported that, for the first month: "It was a seven-day-a-week schedule, with most of the pilots lucky if they got seven hours sleep out of thirty-two." He checked the records of individual fliers: "Lieutenant Donald Ahle flew seven and one-half hours, and in addition had duty for sixteen, and slept eight. Lieutenant Cole Bacon flew seven and one-half, had duty for fourteen and one-half, and slept eight and one-half. Pampering himself, I guess. Lieutenant Clinton Hillman flew nine, had duty for eighteen, and slept eight. Lieutenant Elmer Murphy flew nine, had duty for nineteen, and slept seven. Captain Adolph Loeck flew eight, had duty for sixteen, and slept eight. That's the way it went for all of them. Still, only 1 man out of 160 goofed off. He had been shot down twice in the war, and his nerves simply could not take the weather and the instrument flying.

"Toward the close of the third week, though, the dangerous level had been reached. A couple of crews came in where both the pilot and the copilot had dozed off, only to be awakened by the change in the altitude of the plane. Their fatigue was shown in their irritability, and they were jagging badly on too much coffee. The long hours, their exhaustion and the weather were causing a lot of colds and a lot of fliers' ears. You know how painful a bad ear is in flight? Well, not a guy quit, and a lot of them were being crucified by plugged ears. Finally, in the fifth week, we had seventy-five crews and that gave us enough fliers to space the boys out for some rest. I put them on a vitamin regime about my first day. They bellyached all over the joint, but now, when they don't need vitamins nearly so much, they're around raising hell if the vitamins run short."

There was much bellyaching—most of it, at that time, in the nature of healthy griping that was a way of letting off steam. Later, there would be a considerable morale problem, but this was not evident in the early "cowboy" days of the operation. Typical of the gripes was one that

almost became an international *cause célèbre*. Obviously
in such a hurriedly conceived operation, many of the nice-
ties of living were in short supply. Some who liked ketchup
on their steak did not have it. There was frequently a
shortage of beer and cold soda. One night the crew of a
Gooney Bird, flying in supplies of the French occupation
forces, found that part of their cargo consisted of wine.
This was too much. If the French had to have wine, why
didn't they fly it in themselves? The fliers did not object
to flying milk for the babies of their erstwhile enemies,
but why should the French have wine when the Americans did not even have Coca-Cola? When word of this
reached the French, they were outraged to the point of
sending a delegation to USAFE headquarters with a dietary history of France, to prove that wine was as necessary
to a Frenchman as potatoes to a German, black bread to
a Russian, or ketchup to a Texan. After much grousing in
ready rooms and squadron lounges, the affair blew over.

The airlift was not an all-Air Force operation. The
planes carried what was laid down at Rein-Main to Berlin.
Getting supplies to the departure points was the job of
the Army Transportation Corps, and although less dramatic, this was equally complex. Railroad lines ran from
the seaport at Bremerhaven to Frankfort, but there were
no adequate truck roads from the railhead to the bases,
nor were there staging facilities for thousands of tons of
freight. Truck drivers worked as long and as hard as pilots.

Each ten-ton trailer truck carried a crew of twelve or
fourteen displaced persons—Serbs, Latvians, Estonians,
Lithuanians, Poles—as loaders, commanded by an American corporal or Pfc. When a trailer was backed to the

door of a plane half of the D.P.s jumped in, and the remainder passed sacks of flour or macaroni, dehydrated potatoes, and cases of medicine through what had been designed as a passenger door. Those inside piled the cargo
on the floor of the bare fuselage, and the American supervised the tieing-down. Later, more efficient loading and
unloading procedures would be developed. Over at Fassberg, the British were doing the same thing with coal that
came by rail from the Ruhr. The main difference was that
the American G.I.s and their D.P. crews were white from
head to toe with flour, and the British Tommies and their
D.P. crews were black from head to toe with coal dust.

Because they worked stripped to the waist, it was hard
to tell the G.I.s from the D.P.s. A British officer who came
over to see how the Americans were doing it asked one
American corporal in the bed of a truck, covered with flour
and dust, "Hard work, old man?" "Yah," replied the corporal with characteristic irreverence. Thinking that the
G.I. had said "Ja," the Britisher asked, in careful English,
"How much are the Amedicans paying you chaps?" "I
don't know, sir," the corporal replied. "I'm a corporal and
the 'Amedicans' don't pay me nothin'. The U.S. Army pays
me a regular corporal's pay every month, though."

Even while it was a "cowboy" operation, the life of an
airlift pilot was very different from his usual routine. In
combat operation, fliers were customarily based far behind the lines in adequate—sometimes plush—quarters.
Bomber crews seldom flew more than one mission a day,
usually less. The mission itself was dangerously exciting,
but between missions there was time for rest and facilities
for recreation. At Rein-Main there were no proper quar-

ters for the sudden influx of airlift personnel. A man was lucky to have a cot, and he spent little time in it. Although the actual flying time for the round trip in a C-47 was slightly under four hours, the total elapsed time, including briefing, unloading, and turn around was close to eight hours. In the first hectic weeks crews made two round trips a day. Between flights there was nothing to do except —if a flier was lucky—sleep.

The Gooney Bird period of the airlift was reminiscent of the old "flying by the seat of the pants" days of early aviation. True, there were instruments and radio contact with beacons and control towers. But the planes, the airports, the landing lights, the radar and the electronic control, and communications equipment then available were not adequate for this type of operation. Human stamina and skill were the important ingredients in keeping LeMay's Coal and Feed Company going. Yet, day after day, it kept going and improving.

Major Wilberford, the novice cargo officer, told of a staff meeting that was held four days after the airlift started: "When we got to the point in the meeting where it was necessary to make a forecast on our future performance, I was ready. General Smith called on me. I stood up and said, 'I estimate that by July 20 we'll be flying in 1500 tons every twenty-four hours.' I looked around proudly and everyone was studying me in consternation, for you see, that day, by straining ourselves black in the face, we'd hauled in 384 tons, and to quadruple that amount in a little over two weeks seemed insane. Incidentally, on July 15, we flew 1530 tons into Berlin."

THREE

The Gathering of the Gulls

At 9 A.M. on the sunny Sunday of July 26, 1948, Lt. Colonel Forrest Coon landed his C-54 transport at Bergstrom Field, Texas, home base of the 48th Troop Carrier Squadron. It had been a long trip from Guam, and after two and a half years in the Philippines, he was glad to be home. On this hot day he made a beeline for the well-remembered swimming pool. Before he had dunked a toe the loud speaker crackled: "All personnel report immediately to Operations." A few hours later Col. Coon and the forty-seven other officers and eighty-eight enlisted men of the 48th were winging their nine C-54s toward Frankfort, Germany.

The men and planes of the 54th Troop Carrier Squadron were at their home base in Anchorage, Alaska, when they got the word. They brought along their snowshoes, standard equipment for the Alaskan base, although they would not be needed in Germany. These ended as wall decorations in the 54th's Operations Room at Rein-Main. The 19th Troop Carrier Squadron at Hickam Field Honolulu was one C-54 short. This one had just landed at Brisbane, Australia, when its commander received word to return to Hickam immediately. Pausing only to refuel at its home base, it streaked after its eleven sister ships toward Rein-Main. Another twelve planes of the 20th Troop Carrier Squadron winged from Panama in the Canal Zone.

When he finished talking to LeMay to ask for help from the Air Force, General Clay had called Secretary of State George Marshall in Washington. Could the Secretary get more and bigger planes assigned to USAFE to supplement the Gooney Birds? The result was the gathering of C-54 troop carriers from all corners of the globe at Rein-Main. Within two weeks after the lift started, fifty-four of them had reached Germany. Ultimately, 225 of them would entirely replace the smaller planes, with almost another 100 backing them up in ferrying supplies from the States and training additional crews.

The C-54 was a four-engine plane, known on civilian airlines as the DC-4. It had a load factor of almost ten tons, over three times as great as that of the Gooney Birds. Its cruising speed was 180, against the smaller plane's 170. But it had the same basic fault for airlift work as the C-47; it was a passenger plane, not a freighter. As soon as the larger planes landed at Rein-Main, ground crewmen swarmed aboard to adapt the troop carriers to their new work. Long-range navigational equipment was ripped out, as were the navigator's stool, forward fuselage gas tanks, partitions, troop benches, wash water tanks, and all else not needed to carry food to Berlin. In their places, D.P.s quickly loaded flour, cheese, dehydrated vegetables, boneless meat, and within a few hours from the time that they touched down in Germany, the first of the C-54s joined their smaller sisters on the Berlin run.

The British, too, during the opening weeks of July,

stepped up their activity with four-engine Yorks from England and the first of a few Sunderland flying boats, the largest craft employed on the lift, which landed on a lake in the British sector and were unloaded by lighter. Because their hulls were protected against corrosive salt water, the Sunderlands carried all of the salt to the city. When the lake froze over, the British devised a scheme for carrying this corrosive substance in pannier-like containers, very much as salt had been carried in ancient times by camel caravans. Although much is heard of Yankee ingenuity, it was also the British who solved the problem of carrying liquid fuel to the beleaguered city—a difficult and dangerous cargo to carry in drums—by hiring civilian tanker planes to fly kerosene, gasoline, and diesel oil in bulk.

It is not clear just when the decision was made to try to meet all of Berlin's requirements by air. Initially, Clay had asked LeMay to ferry only enough supplies for the occupation troops, but he promptly put Howley's experts to work to determine the minimum tonnage of food, medicines, fuel, and other necessities that would be required to maintain life in the city. Berlin normally imported 15,500 tons a day for personal and industrial use. If life were reduced to bare essentials it was estimated that the city could get by with 4,500 tons a day—4000 for the Berliners and 500 for the occupation forces. On July 20, Clay flew to Washington with these and other figures for a meeting with President Truman, cabinet members, the Joint Chiefs of Staff, and the National Security Council. The President's flat statement, "We are going to stay in Berlin," was presumably the decision to try to completely supply the city by air.

In its second phase, during the first half of the summer of 1948, the airlift was still a "cowboy operation," albeit it got bigger and more frenzied. On the ground, Rein-Main (which the G.I.s dubbed "Rein-Mud") came to resemble a boom town of gold rush days. Expanded facilities for the airlift—living quarters, hangars, warehouses, fire stations—were being hammered together in a sea of mud, through which army engineers were pushing roads and railway spurs. G.I.s and D.P.s alike waded through mud in the newly created truck park to reach their trailer trucks, and around the park spread a new city of tents and huts to house the D.P.s.

Two of the C-54 squadrons were from the Navy, manned by naval fliers. When they arrived, the water on the field at Rein-Main was almost up to the knees, and as they landed the planes sent a wave of spray flying high in the air. After taxiing to the hardstand, the door of the first plane opened and the natty naval officers, in well-creased blues and highly polished shoes, looked dubiously down at the water and the sodden Air Force officers who had come out to greet them.

"General, sir," said the pilot, "would you just tell me one thing. Are we on land or at sea?"

"Why," said General Smith, "we ordered this just for you. We want the Navy to feel at home."

At the other end, the metaled runway at Templehof soon started to break down under the constant hammering of the heavily laden airlift planes arriving in rapid succession. The runway had not been designed for such punishment. To counter this, a labor force of 225 German civilians was organized for a wild maintenance operation. Armed

with shovels, and pushing wheelbarrows loaded with asphalt and sand, this crew lined the edges of the runway.
As soon as a plane landed, they scurried on to the strip
to repair the damage, scrambling off three minutes later to
avoid being hit by the next plane. Working round the
clock, they managed to give some semblance of a runway
to the deteriorating landing strip while army engineers
built two additional hard-surfaced runways.

Despite much frenzy and confusion, tonnages went
steadily upward. This was due partly to more planes,
partly to improved loading and unloading practices. The
planes, designed to carry passengers, could never be loaded
with freight efficiently—it had to be carried aboard piece
by piece, manually, and tied down with straps to keep it
from bouncing around the cabin. But many little tricks
were developed to speed up the operation to the point
where the original loading and unloading times were cut
by more than 50 percent. The most effective trick was to
establish a competition between the crews of D.P.s in which
outstanding performers were rewarded with cigarettes. One
crew of twelve D.P.s established a record by loading twenty
thousand pounds of coal into a C-54 in five minutes and
forty-five seconds, for which they were rewarded with a
whole pack of cigarettes per man. Considering the black-
market value of a pack of cigarettes, this made them the
richest D.P.s in Germany.

When the scarcity of flying crews eased off late in July,
other shortages made continued operation touch and go.
As one operations officer put it when recalling this phase
of the airlift, "We didn't have enough spare parts in
Europe to rebuild the ass end of a Piper Cub." Some were

little things that few would think of, like windshield wipers. USAFE's six months reserve of these was used up during the first two weeks of the lift. Before spare parts depots could be organized and equipped engines and tires had to be flown from the United States to keep the planes in the air. Gasoline was a problem throughout the summer. The airlift would have been grounded within three weeks had not three tankers, already at sea headed for other destinations, been deflected to Bremerhaven whence the fuel was brought 240 miles to Rein-Main in tank cars.

In the air, conditions were somewhat less hectic. By mid-July, Berlin and Rein-Main were thronged with newspaper, magazine, and radio reporters. All of the stories they cabled or shipped home dealt with the drama and danger and derring-do that surrounded the brave and dedicated fliers who were ferrying life-giving supplies to the beleaguered city. In fact, most of the principal problems that had to be licked to make the lift a success were on the ground, not in the air. To the outsider, the flying was the dramatic aspect of the operation, and there was danger —although most of the seventy-nine fatalities of the airlift were on the ground. Possibly, at this time, there was too much derring-do. But the real problems had to do with ground operations: the creation of airport facilities, of approach roads, of spare parts depots, of facilities and systems for maintenance and ground control, of airport lighting, of loading and unloading, of efficient briefing and turn-around procedures.

One complication of flying during this period was the mixture of Gooney Birds and the larger C-54s. Until the smaller planes were phased out of the operation, all proce-

dures had to be based on their slower speed; under the
conditions it was not possible to fly some planes at 170 mph
and others at 180. The planes were dispatched in blocks,
three of which made two round trips a day. There was
an interval of three minutes between the takeoff time of
each plane in the block, the same headway as the New
York subway. This involved a landing or a takeoff at
Templehof every ninety seconds. The planes were stag-
gered at 500 foot intervals of elevations from 5000 to 6500
feet. Much was made, in the press, of the "narrow and dangerous" corridors to which the planes were confined. Actually, pilots were more concerned with the vertical leeway
of 500 feet than with the horizontal restriction of twenty
miles. As one said, "Us peasants ought to be able to stay
in a twenty-mile-lane unless we're crocked, and I don't
want to be up there with any crocked peasants."

Part of the "cargo" flown during the summer were press
corerspondents and V.I.P.s, the former to report to the
nation on this dramatic undertaking and the latter, presumably, to satisfy their curiosity. Almost every correspondent sent back a story of his personal flight to Berlin. Most
of them made it a tense and exciting experience, fraught
with nerve-tingling danger. Quentin Reynolds, for instance, thus described the takeoff of the C-47 in which he
made the trip: "We start to roll. Gerry isn't sitting back
relaxed. The skin is tight on the back of his neck. The
plane gathers momentum slowly. It creaks and groans with
the effort. We're halfway down the runway now, and the
plane feels as logy as a sackful of wet wheat. I feel I want
to lift it by main force, and after what seems an eternity,
it lurches a bit, and we're airborne. The pilot still isn't re-

laxed. He won't be until he gets over those hills at Fulda. Slowly, agonizingly, the plane climbs and then, after some five minutes, Gerry raises his head and sits back." A well-written description of an exciting experience—but in fact, DC-3s, civilian counterparts of the Gooney Birds, had been making such takeoffs under similar conditions with equal loads for fourteen years on commercial airlines. The operation was purely routine.

Other correspondents stressed the menace of the Russians. This was surely a psychological hazard, and it never developed into a real one. Shortly after the airlift started, the Soviets began a campaign of scare propaganda presumably designed to intimidate the Western fliers. They formally announced that on certain days there would be anti-aircraft practice in the vicinity of the corridors. There were numerous Russian airfields adjacent to the corridors, crowded with Yak fighters, and these frequently flew formations near the corridors and at the same altitudes as the airlift planes. But there was no instance of Russian planes challenging the airlift planes. At no time during the lift did the Russians attempt to interfere with its operation. The explanation was probably that, from the first, the Allies had taken a determined stand on the air corridors, insisting that this form of access be a matter of formal written agreement and that procedures be strictly adhered to. This was one of very few instances in which the Westerners were tough; and in all such cases, the Soviets were surprisingly docile.

One personal description of a flight to Berlin was written by Paul Fisher, reporter for the industrial house organ of United Aircraft Corporation, which made the Pratt & Whitney engines that powered the airlift planes. Fisher's account may be considered as a good description of a typical flight in fair weather. After explaining that the plane in which he flew was from the 54th Troop Carrier Squadron, normally based at Elmendorf Field, Anchorage, Alaska, and that it still flew the bright red pennant of the north country to make it more visible in the event of a forced landing in the snow, Fisher continued:

"Lieutenant Victor Wiebeck, a native of Adrian, Mich., was piloting 609. He had flown both B-17s and B-24s on missions over Germany during the war. Five times his destination for today, Berlin, had been a bomb target. Today he followed an old practice of his own; two hours before the flight he had gone to his aircraft and checked carefully with the ground crew. He knew that number three generator was out, that the autopilot was inoperative, and that the left wheel strut was leaking air. He had swung his 215 pounds of bone and muscle all over the aircraft, checking here, checking there, chatting with this ground crewman, interrogating the next. And finally he double-checked the lashings on the macaroni; he said that he disliked loose macaroni in the cockpit.

"At 1:55 o'clock, as the thirty-ninth C-54 in the noon block, he began taxiing his plane north. His was the seventh ship in the line. His copilot, Lieutenant George Jones, had the check list ready and shortly Wiebeck's staccato voice was demanding of him, 'Cowl flaps open?' 'Open.' 'Tank selectors on main?' 'On main.' 'Cross feeds off?' 'Off.' And on down the checks.

"Exactly at 2:15, Wiebeck opened the throttle, the big Skymaster surged forward, and the instant it broke away from the ground, Wiebeck reduced his engine speed and manifold pressure. For the next few minutes he followed the prescribed climb and course procedure to reach his assigned altitude of 6500 feet. He had picked up the Darmstadt beacon almost at once. As he climbed, the last pockets of the morning storm vanished; ahead the sunlight was sucked into the huge cumulous formations.

"The hand of the air speed indicator held at 170 miles an hour. Darmstadt was passed. Jones had picked up the Aschaffenburg beacon and reset his radio. Below, perhaps 2000 feet, a cloud hung thick and rumpled. Wiebeck turned his head.

" 'You'd think all the traffic would tear these clouds to bits,' he said. 'I've seen when it looked like that had happened.'

"Jones turned to grin. 'Yeh, Vic,' he said. 'And I've heard you say that on perfectly clear days all the dirty weather gathers in the corridor.'

" 'Well,' Wiebeck said, 'it seems so.'

" 'We're by Aschaffenburg,' the copilot said. Motioning downward with his thumb he added, 'Fulda.' [Fulda was the radio range beacon marking the entrance to the southern corridor.]

" 'In about eight minutes start looking down and to the right,' said Wiebeck. 'We'll be over in Russian territory. See if you see what I always see on good days.'

"The country below swept in rolling landscape like the farming lands of Pennsylvania or northern Missouri. There was one curious absence; the lonely farmhouses and barns did not dot the earth as they do in the United States. Instead, huddled together, lay the red-tiled roofs of the vil-

lages where farmers live together, trudging or bicycling to
their fields. Nowhere were there cattle. The fields show
brown and rich to the edge of the forests the Germans so
carefully cultivate; indeed, the forests had the planted look
of well-tended corn.

"Directly below, suddenly, an enormous field was
marked by an odd pattern; thousands of furrows crossed
and re-crossed, and the earth was churned furiously and
without thought. A second look made one doubt one's
eyes; those were not furrows, for the earth was simply
flattened. They led toward a wood denser than the other
forests and there disappeared.

"Wiebeck was leaning back. 'See it?' he asked.

" 'What was it?'

" 'Tank tracks. Russians probably have a tank division
in those woods. Those tracks were fresh today.' He studied
his instrument panel. 'Show you something else in about
eighteen minutes,' he said.

"The C-54 plunged into an enormous white cloud. A
lace moisture formed on the cockpit glass and began running in rivulets. Neither the altimeter nor the air-speed indicator bobbled—both remained at their true figures of
6500 feet and 170 miles an hour. Below the Skymaster,
three lanes of planes moved toward Templehof in the
ceaseless pattern of the airlift.

"After a time, Wiebeck said, 'Off to the right.' There
lay an airfield. Scattered around its edges were scores of
Russian fighters.

" 'Probably all Yaks,' Wiebeck observed. 'Look like Yaks
to me anyhow. I guess the Stalin boys aren't flying today.
Appears like the full field of planes is down there.'

" 'Vic, I got Templehof sometime back,' Jones said.

" 'Routine?'

" 'Sounds routine from here.'

" 'I don't know what Goering and Hitler were thinking of at Templehof,' Wiebeck mused. 'Got a damned seven-story apartment just where you let down to hit the Temple-hof strip. If I'd known what I was going through on the airlift, I would have managed to drop some eggs on that building, believe me.'

"Shortly, Wiebeck began his left-hand turn in the pattern of let-down for the Templehof landing. He swung over the Wedding beacon, cut right, and circled toward the apartment building. Below, the immense city lay, broken and mottled, walls leaning drunkenly, unroofed buildings gaping, the most shattered capital in the world. Now he was on his last leg. Far to his left stood a 400 foot chimney, untouched by the devastation. The sweeping pattern of Templehof's field was spread below, its mile-long administration and hangar building curving along with the ramp. Wiebeck was over his apartment, and dropping down, he touched on the power, straightened out, and smoothed out for the landing. As he started his taxi run, a jeep, with a big board painted in diagonal maroon and yellow stripes, whipped in front of him. It bore the sign, 'Follow me.' Wiebeck's C-54 clicked along behind the small guide, pulled up at its assigned stand, and almost at once a tractor backed a trailer against 609 and seventeen Germans, many of them middle-aged, began the job of unloading the aircraft."

Lieutenant Wiebeck's last comment on the trip, according to Paul Fisher, was made over a cup of coffee and a

doughnut. Looking up at the apartment house he remarked, "If I had me a BB gun damned if I wouldn't
shoot out a window, at least."

The most important aspect of the flight to Berlin, from
the pilot's standpoint, was to exactly follow the prescribed
flying procedure. When he left the ground, the pilot followed his takeoff heading until he attained an altitude of
900 feet and then set a course for the Darmstadt radio
beacon, which he was required to reach at an altitude of
3000 feet. Here he turned on the course for the Aschaffenburg beacon, continuing to climb until he reached his prescribed altitude. From the Aschaffenburg beacon, the pilot
set a course of 33° to the Fulda Range, forty-five miles
away. This was his last directional guide until he reached
Berlin. As he approached the Fulda Range, he listened for
the report of the pilot of the plane just ahead of him, who
reported the time as he passed over Fulda. He must adjust
his speed to pass over Fulda exactly three minutes after
the preceding plane. He was now in the corridor and on
his own for the next forty minutes, carefully maintaining
speed and altitude and allowing for drift by dead reckon-
ing. Exactly forty minutes after he passed the Fulda Range
Station, he switched his radio to the Templehof Field Control Station, which immediately reported his time in relation to the preceding plane and gave him a course to the
Wedding beacon. He gradually reduced his speed to 140
mph and descended to cross the Wedding beacon, where
he turned on a downwind leg and descended to 1500 feet.
Six minutes before the final approach, if the weather was
fine, Templehof Field Control turned him over to the
tower which guided him to his final landing.

In talking to Templehof control, Wiebeck's copilot identified himself as Big Easy 39, Big because the plane was a C-54, Easy because the flight was eastbound, 39 because that was the number of the plane in the block. If the plane had been a C-47 it would have been Little Easy 39. On the return trip, the plane became Big Willie 39—indicating that it was westbound. A C-47 going in the same direction would have been Little Willie.

Another correspondent reported on an equally uneventful flight except that in his case a Russian fighter came up and flew beside the plane, at some distance, doing simple aerobatics—to show off. The pilot commented, "They mean no harm." On the return trip this pilot was carrying a bunch of flowers that had been presented to him at Templehof. Berliners, particularly children, took delight in giving the fliers flowers to show their appreciation of the airlift, an act which both pleased and embarrassed the Americans. When the recipient carried them into the squadron lounge some wag always quipped, "Getting married?" In this case the pilot was one of the fortunate few whose wife had come over. At the end of the flight she was waiting for him with a car, like any suburban housewife. The only untoward incident of the flight had been a collision above the clouds with a bird which splattered on the plexiglass windshield of the cabin. As the pilot went off to make his routine report to intelligence the copilot called, "Don't forget to tell them that the Russians sent a bird up after us."

In fair weather, the flight was purely routine, but fair weather was not characteristic of Berlin. One meteorologist figured that if all the airports of the United States were listed in terms of desirability from the standpoint of weather, Pittsburgh would be at the bottom. But compared to Central European airports, Pittsburgh would be at the top of the list—and of the European airports, Berlin was near the bottom. Even in July, normally a good month for weather, more than half of the flights were made on instruments. In foul weather, the close tolerances made the end of the flight somewhat perilous. The distance between Gatow and Templehof airports in Berlin was only 100 flying seconds, and there was always the danger that a British plane slightly off course would meet an American plane slightly off course, in mid-air.

To relieve the monotony of flying down the corridor, pilots at this phase of the airlift chatted with each other by radio. In the squadron lounges their wisecracks were repeated *ad nauseum,* like the one about the flier who, when the tower told him, "If you read the tower flap your wings," replied, "Roger, tower, and if you read the ship flap your tower." One day, as the boys were talking to each other, a voice from the blue suddenly interrupted to say, "This is Colonel So-and-so. I order you to stop that chatter." Immediately there was a few seconds of dead silence until another voice said softly, "I wonder if he ral-ly, ral-ly is a colonel?" None of this was very funny, but under the circumstances of fatigue and monotony, anything that lightened the load was worth repeating.

The British were lost in wonder at the informality of American communications. When American planes started to fly from Fassberg, the English controllers could not get used to the irreverent comments from American pilots awaiting takeoff, such as, "Just give me the woid and I'll make like a boid."

A favorite story was the one about Squeaky Mary, a British WAAF at Gatow airport, who came by her nickname because of her high-pitched voice. Whenever she told a pilot his course in her squeaky treble he answered in an equally squeaky imitation. One day when Mary called the field at Templehof an American answered, briskly, "Shoot, Luke, you're faded." For a moment Mary was nonplused, then she explained: "You see, it's been so long since I've had close contact with Americans—it's good to be at it again."

When American planes started to use the British base at Fassberg they shared with their allies the special problem of flying coal. This was a necessity in Berlin, even in July, for utilities, transportation, and bakeries. Coal, which had never been flown before, was a pernicious cargo. Its dust in concentration was highly inflammable, and it was virtually impossible to prevent it from fouling up the instruments. At first it was carried in ordinary G.I. fabric duffle bags, but these were porous, and the dust problem was acute. The bags were wet down to try to cope with this, but the water added to the weight. Finally, five-ply paper bags were devised which, although not so sturdy, solved the dust problem. Although they were good for only three trips, against the duffle bags' twenty, the saving in weight and clean up time made it worthwhile to buy half a million new paper coal sacks every month.

Early in the lift, somebody got the bright idea that coal might be dropped from a low altitude to save landing and takeoff time in Berlin. The idea apparently came from a fairly high level because on the day it was tried, in an open field near Frankfort, a sizable gallery of brass was on hand to observe the results. A C-54 flew low over the target circle on the field and slowed down to near stalling speed while a special crew in the cabin started to push out bags of coal. The bags hit the target accurately and promptly burst into shreds as the coal was splintered into dust. A black cloud of coal dust rose and spread to settle over the landscape, leaving several chicken colonels looking as though they were made up to play black-face in a high school minstrel.

Somewhat more successful was an idea conceived by a British sergeant whose hobby was falconry. The field at Fassberg was plagued by large flocks of sparrows which dashed against windshields and flew into propellers at take-off. The falconer sent to England for a few hunting birds. What the RAF could not do with its planes, the falcons did in a few hours. As soon as they were released, the sparrows went elsewhere.

As the summer progressed, the press of the free world marveled that the airlift continued, with the steady beat of a metronome, to land a plane load of supplies in Berlin every three minutes. True, it did not yet supply the minimum needs that had been established for the city, about 135,000 tons a month, but if only the summer weather conditions could continue year round, the lift might reach its goal. But everybody knew that ahead were months of foul flying weather when the lift could not maintain its frantic pace. Typical of the profound forecasts, was a comment in *Time*, "But it was obvious that Operation Vittles could not be carried on at summer rate when winter comes. In the long run, the siege would have to be lifted from the outside." *U.S. News & World Report* concurred and editorialized that the impossibility of bringing in enough coal would bring the crisis to a head with the advent of cold weather. In London, the *New Statesman* said, "Every expert knows that aircraft, despite their immense psychological value, cannot be relied upon to provision Berlin in the winter months." But, like the bee who did not know that it was scientifically impossible for him to fly, the airlift fliers droned on, oblivious to the fact that what they were trying to do was impossible.

FOUR

The Summer of Uncertainty

A battered alarm clock sounded shrilly. Frau Schultz reached out a fumbling hand in the dark and turned it off, then rose to sit on the side of the bed, rubbing sleep from her eyes. *"Was ist los, Mutter?"* asked the drowsy voice of her husband.

"It's two o'clock. The electricity comes on tonight from two to six. We must get the work done. Elsa! Elsa, you get at the ironing."

Behind a blanket that screened off her cot in the corner eighteen-year-old Elsa was already hustling into her clothes. She called to her mother, "I have to get my hair done. The beauty parlor is going to open while the current is on. Josef promised to do me if I got there early."

"So your father will wear wrinkled shirts while you have waves in your hair? First comes the ironing."

"Let her go," said Herr Schultz. "A few more wrinkles don't matter to me. If anyone's going to look better, let it be Elsa."

With a hurried kiss of thanks for her father Elsa dashed out into the dark as life started in the Schultz household in the hours before dawn.

To some Berliners, in the summer of 1948, the vagaries

of household electric power made life more difficult than the restricted, monotonous diet. The equipment that the Russians had ripped from Berlin's biggest power plant when they first occupied the city had never been replaced. Prior to the blockade, most of the power had come from the eastern sector; and now this was denied to residents of the western parts of the city. The limited generating capacity that was left to the West ran the street transportation during the day—after a fashion—and allowed very limited current for industrial use and provided household and commercial power for different sections of the city for two- to four-hour periods at various times of night. To be fair to all, the periods were rotated. A particular neighborhood might get current from nine to twelve one week, from twelve to three the next, and from three to six the third.

The regulations regarding the use of power changed from time to time. Every day new ordinances were published in the newspapers which nobody understood. An attempt was made to ration use at sub-meters, and all were afraid of using up their allotments and sitting for a month in total darkness. They wondered whether, if they ran over, the meter reader could be bribed. One newspaper ad proclaimed, "I herewith announce that I will not be responsible for any debts incurred by my wife. Likewise, my wife is solely responsible for her own consumption of gas and electricity."

As part of her predawn chores, Frau Schultz heated water and saved a thermos for her husband to shave. She placed covered bowls of soup under the bed clothes where body heat would keep them warm, and there was something called "a blockade blitz pill," a variety of canned heat, that would warm a small pan of liquid, but these were in scarce supply. Elsewhere in the city, operations were being performed in hospitals on a schedule fitted to the power supply. Movies played in the middle of the night to audiences that walked halfway across the dark city to see them. Concerts and lectures were held by candlelight. When the current was off, dentists' wives generated power for drills by pumping bicycle wheels.

At the beginning of the summer, the most frustrating aspect of day-to-day living was the uncertainty and confusion. Everybody wanted to know what was happening. There was an eager search for news, or an exchange of rumors that passed for news. A schoolteacher wrote, "The newspapers were read with nervous haste and violent discussions of their contents took place." A nurse recalled, "Excited groups were debating everywhere." The *Telegraf* reported on June 27 that so many groups were holding discussions in the streets that all Berlin looked like London's Hyde Park. One public opinion surveyor compared the attitude of the people with that which prevailed at the start of the war. "The public mood was very fluid; everything was uncertain and in a state of suspended animation . . . Nobody had an exact picture of the situation. Everything was possible."

The Russians used this avid interest in news to increase their propaganda and made wild charges against the Western Allies. "Food riots sweep West Berlin as thousands are thrown out of work," blared their radio. "Babies are dying from lack of milk," screamed their press. An epidemic was imminent, they said, as a result of the stoppage of pumps in the sewage disposal system due to lack of electricity.

"The water supply of the western sectors has also failed in various areas." None of this was true, but the water rumor caused a temporary water shortage as a result of hoarding. And with it all went the old rumors, intensified. The Western Allies were on the verge of leaving the city. Russian troops and armor were massed on its outskirts, waiting to move in.

To keep the people confused and stirred up, the Socialist Unity Party sent in "shock troop speakers" and "agitation autos" from the Soviet sector. The speakers joined groups on busy street corners to attack the Western military governments and quote editorials from the Communist press. The autos, filled with members of the Communist Free German Youth, cruised the western sectors handing out leaflets.

Initially, the blockade was a secondary concern of most Berliners. Many felt that it was just another dispute among the occupying powers that did not directly concern them. They knew that food for thirty days was available and took for granted that before it was exhausted, this particular dispute would be settled and some new source of controversy would come to the fore in the unending conflict among the foreigners. Of more immediate concern was the confusion over money.

For months before the blockade, the Western powers had been trying to get a Russian agreement to a system of currency reform for all of Germany, as a means of fighting the inflation which was hampering the German economy. The Russians refused unless they could print the new money for East Germany from a duplicate set of plates— an impossible condition because the Soviets could then print as much money as they pleased. On June 18, six days before the blockade became total, the Western occupation authorities announced a new west mark for West Germany, not including Berlin, that would be worth ten of the old marks. The next day Marshal Sokolovsky declared, "Bank notes issued in the western occupation zones of Germany are not being admitted for circulation in the Soviet occupation zone of Germany and in Berlin, which is part of the Soviet occupation zone." This was the first "official" announcement that the Russians now claimed all of Berlin as a part of their zone.

On June 22, the Soviets announced a new east mark and proclaimed it the only legal tender for East Germany and all of Berlin. In fact, these "new" marks were battered old marks with a thumbnail size stamp glued on. These were shortly dubbed "wallpaper marks." To add to the griefs of Berliners, the stamps readily fell off, so that there was no evidence that the bill had been changed for a new one. The Russians tried to force the city government to accept an order that theirs was to be the only currency for all Berlin. They packed the gallery and corridors of the City Hall with Communist goons when the Assembly met to consider the order. When the democratic majority of the Assembly voted that Russian orders applied only to the Soviet sector, the leaders of the Social Democrats were beaten up while the Communist zone police looked on.

Meanwhile, the Western authorities had anticipated the Soviet move to impose the new east marks on Berlin and, in a cloak-and-dagger operation of strictest secrecy, had flown in 250,000,000 new west marks in cases marked "whisky," "gin" and "brandy." On June 23, they broke open these cases of supposed liquor and announced that the new west marks would be legal tender in their sectors of the city, although east marks would also be accepted.

It is understandable that Berliners were confused and worried. The Russians told them that they must change their money for "wallpaper marks." The Western authorities told them that they should change for new west marks. They lost either way. The city government, and the treasury, were in the Russian sector, and all city employees were paid in east marks. The Russians promptly decreed that it was a crime for a Berliner to have west marks in his possession. The Western currency was confiscated when found in the eastern zone and its owners fined or jailed. Yet the Berliners wanted west marks which soon sold at a premium of two to one and later at more than three to one. This was the "official" rate, although there was no official exchange. Such transactions usually were made on the black market where the ratio was much higher in favor of the west mark.

Recalling the beginning of the blockade, a business man later wrote, "The news of the total blockade at first was lost in the confusion which the currency reform brought with it. We were all so occupied with questions as to where and how we could change our money, should we also change money in East Berlin, will we have enough money to get along, and so on that, at first, the blockade scarcely seemed important."

Another reason for the Berliners' refusal o accept the blockade as a serious threat was expressed by the Deputy Mayor of Berlin, who told the Assembly: "I would understand it if even in our own circle we would hesitate to look the Medusa head of this emergency straight in the eye. It is something so unheard of, something so unthinkable, something so unprecedented, that in a peacetime city, or a large portion of a city, over 2,000,000 inhabitants should no longer receive the necessities of life. For this reason an inner sense makes us defend ourselves against such a possibility, and we think instinctively that such things cannot be serious, and the threat must somehow be averted and that such a possibility will simply not be tolerated by the world."

As the days passed, more and more Berliners started to look the Medusa head in the eye as the reality of the blockade was brought home. To some, it came more quickly than others. Mothers who realized that there would be no more fresh milk for their babies were, perhaps, among the first to appreciate the seriousness of the situation, an acceptance that spread more widely when the Berlin worker read posters in the subway which announced that, henceforth, trains would not run after six P.M.

One analyst noted a three-phase reaction on the part of the people. At the beginning, there was a period when most people did not recognize that a crisis existed that affected them personally. They believed that the blockade was merely another incident in the dispute among the occupying powers, which did not concern Germans. When it became clear that the Russians were serious in attempting to gobble up the whole city, there was a period of doubt and hesitation. Would the Western powers resist? Was there a chance that Berlin would remain free or would the Westerners leave Berliners to their fates at the hands of the Russians? Would the hardships induced by the blockade prove unendurable? Finally, there came the time when an increasing number of people decided that resistance was possible and that there was hope of avoiding Soviet domination. An aspect of this final phase was a wave of anger at the Russians which rose during the summer to partially replace the earlier fear.

A public opinion survey made during the second phase indicated that forty percent of the people expected war, sixty percent did not; twenty-five percent expected that the Western powers would leave and the Soviets "just walk in"; about a third expected the airlift to succeed; two-thirds expected it to fail. As the monotonous drone of the engines overhead continued, faith and hope increased for the Berliners. By the end of July, they had more confidence in the Westerners than they had before the blockade started. In a survey made in May, 1948, the question, "Do you think that the Americans will stay in Berlin as long as they stay in Germany?" was answered in the affirmative by only seventy-three percent of the respondents; by July's end, the percentage had increased to eighty-nine percent.

The strongest factor in convincing Berliners that resistance was possible was the airlift, for it tended to dispel the fear that the Western powers might leave, the fear of hunger, and, because the airlift appeared to be a nonviolent way of combating the blockade, the fear of war. This last fear flared up momentarily, ten days after the airlift started, when explosions were heard in the American sector. Few Germans knew that it was an American tradition to celebrate the Fourth of July with fireworks.

A secretary recalled how the pessimism of her father was

allayed. "Then came the day when the airlift started. Father naturally didn't believe it. Therefore he rode to Templehof on his bicycle. He was away a long time. When he came home he said, 'They're actually doing it! They're flying food to Berlin. But they won't be able to bring in enough. Think of this huge city with its millions of people!' " The trend of morale from uncertainty to confidence was expressed in this half-humorous shorthand: "First day—go to Zehlendorf. 'Amis' still there. Am calmed. Tenth day—dried potatoes, dried vegetables, tinned meat, egg powder. I'm still calmer. Thirtieth—coal from the heavens. Planes like clockwork. Ear plugs by my bed."

The state of popular feeling in mid-July was summarized by an editorial in the *Telegraf:* "What does the man in the street say? 'This, too, will pass.' 'His' streetcar line, too, will run again some day. He turns up his coat collar, presses his hat further down on his forehead and tramps home. It is raining—the way it does every day. A whole caravan tramps through the rain. Worn heels, shoes with holes in them, no raincoats. Nobody complains; everybody grits his teeth. 'This, too, will pass . . .' This expression of the man on the street may be considered characteristic of the behavior of the Berliners during these critical days. They don't feel themselves to be heroes at all. That's the way it is, and it must be endured."

The American Army ran a series of public opinion surveys about the attitude of the people in Berlin to the policies of the occupation forces. A sampling of some of the individual reactions follows.

" 'We are accustomed to trouble,' says one woman, when she hears the news about the reduction in the gas ration.

'We will take anything with good humor. We will even become "raw food eaters" if it must be. We get the meat already prepared in cans anyway; it does not need to be cooked. That way one saves gas.' Another housewife thinks it will certainly be difficult to get along with the reduced gas ration. She has already thought out what she should do; wash the dishes in cold water and put one pot on top of another when cooking. . . . And once again the people who live alone are hit hardest. For them there is scarcely enough gas to prepare coffee. 'I have made an arrangement with my neighbor for us to cook together,' says one woman. 'My neighbor also lives alone. That way perhaps we'll get along all right. No, I'm far from losing courage on that account.'

"The same sentiments are expressed by a resident of Neukolln. He is standing at a streetcar stop reading a newspaper. Over him there is the constant sound of aircraft engines. Whenever another plane comes roaring over, he stops reading, takes off his glasses and looks up at the sky. Everybody else is doing the same thing. 'They are bringing the flour for the white rolls,' he says, and smiles. It's seldom that one sees someone smile. . . . There's a ray of light in the midst of power stoppages, transit limitations, and gas restrictions."

The American correspondents who thronged Berlin during the summer sent back stories which created two prevalent misconceptions in the minds of those in the States. The first was the impression that *all* Berliners were ready to lay down their lives in defense of democracy. When the blockade started, there was a small group of active pro-democrats in the western sectors, including the leaders of the Social Democrat Party and of the independent labor unions. There was a smaller group of pro-Communists. The great majority of the people were uncommitted. As time passed and more people got mad, the ranks of the first group swelled while those of the last shrank, until the leaders who were willing to fight for freedom could assemble a crowd estimated at three hundred thousand in a mass meeting before the gutted Reichstag building. Unquestionably, the stand of the Berliners was heroic, but the majority of them remained interested in their own welfare and the welfare of their city, rather than an Anglo-American or a Russian political philosophy.

The attitude of some was expressed by an architect who was quoted as saying: "Three years ago it was possible to talk of working with the Allies because they were working with each other. We were told that we had to do two things really: be against militarism and be against Nazism. But that is not enough now. Now in the West we must be against the Russians and in the East we must be against the Americans. Wherever you happen to be that is the only way to prove yourself to be a true 'democrat.' So I say no, there is nothing for us Germans to do but be neutral and wait until Stalin and Truman finish playing their own little game."

The second misconception that was conveyed by the correspondents on the scene was that Berliners loved their Anglo-American protectors. There was very little love for any foreigners in Berlin. The people hated and feared the Russians; they merely resented, and in some cases disliked, the Americans and English. They did not want the "Amis" to go home and leave them at the mercy of the Russians.

What they really wanted was for everybody to go home and let them mind their own affairs. Considering what had transpired from 1939 to 1945, their resentment at the occupying forces might be considered unreasonable. But the Berliners did not consider themselves responsible for the war nor for the atrocities of the Nazis. They had been beaten; they had suffered; now could they please be allowed to work out their own destiny and regain at least a measure of a civilized life.

It must be sadly admitted that the conduct of some members of the occupying forces gave grounds for resentment. There was a small minority of American officers and civilians whose attitude was reminiscent of the British in the "Inja" of Rudyard Kipling's day. They were the lordly Raj; the Germans were the lowly natives who must be kept in their places. The best of the undamaged housing in better class suburbs had been requisitioned for the use of the occupying officers and their families. There were few limitations of the diet of the Westerners; 500 tons a day of the supplies that were flown in were earmarked for the 25,000 foreigners, as opposed to a goal of 4,000 tons for 2,000,000 Germans. Much valuable consumer goods could be bought from the destitute Berliners for a pittance; many returning American families flew out grand pianos, sets of silver, and treasured china. The foreigners had their country clubs and their messes where juicy steaks were always available, and wine and whisky flowed plentifully at tax-free prices. For years, after they returned to the States, some American wives looked back longingly on the "good old days" in Berlin when they could hire a college graduate maid, speaking three languages, for the equivalent of four or five dollars a week. In the face of this double standard, it is not to be wondered that there was some resentment on the part of the Berliners.

This resentment toward the occupying forces in general did not apply to the airlift. Before the end of the summer the airlift has become *volkstümlich*. Freely translated, this means that it had become part of the community. Berliners took pride in it as though it were their own accomplishment and studied the daily tonnage reports in the newspapers like sporting event box scores. Watching the planes land at Templehof became a favorite recreation. Each day the crowds increased until there were sometimes ten thousand people on Berlinerstrasse, bordering the field.

A Sunday event was a picnic at Lake Havel to watch the big British Sunderland flying boats hit the water. Many spectators brought gifts for the fliers—flowers by the armload and treasured pieces of Meissen ware and silver, things that could have provided their owners with a touch of comfort if sold on the black market. School children made little gifts for the fliers, and one correspondent noted that almost every RAF pilot at Gatow wore a small, knitted amulet that had been made by a German child.

An event that seemed to break down the barrier that had existed between the Berliners and the Anglo-American occupation forces was the carsh of a C-47 on July 24, in which its crew of two were killed. The plane plunged into two houses near Templehof, setting them afire. Although none of the residents were fatally injured, the Russians sought to make capital of the incident by propagandizing that the unsafe flying practices of the airlift were endangering the lives of Berliners. This attempt to use the

deaths of two young men for propaganda purposes back-
fired and aroused the ire of all Berliners, who responded
with a flood of sympathy and appreciation for the Americans. When a newspaper account of the tragedy mentioned
that both fliers were the fathers of small children, one
reader sent in twenty marks and asked the paper to start
a fund raising campaign for the children. Another name-
less Berliner put a plaque at the site of the crash which
read:

> Two American fliers became victims of the Berlin
> blockade here. You gave your lives for us! The Ber-
> liners of the west sectors will never forget you. We
> stand deeply moved on this spot which has been dedi-
> cated to your death. Once we were enemies, and yet
> you gave your lives for us. We are now doubly obli-
> gated to you.

For weeks the plaque was kept decorated, by unknown
hands, with fresh flowers. The location is now the site of
a modern monument to all the casualties of the airlift.

The basic diet of the western sectors was controlled by
ration cards which still provided different quantities of
calories for various classes, depending upon their energy
needs. It was, during the summer, slightly lower in calories
than that of the Soviet sector, but the food that was flown
in provided a better-balanced diet nutritionally. High pro-
tein foods such as meat, fish, and cheese were limited, but
somewhat more plentiful than in East Berlin. The fish
was mostly salted and the meat canned. When one large
shipment of canned beef was flown in, bearing a trade-
mark of a man on a horse, the Russians quickly propagan-

dized that the Berliners were being fed horsemeat. No
bread was flown in, and all flour was allotted to bakeries,
where it could be used with more economy of precious
coal than in home baking. Milk was available only in
powdered form, and all vegetables were dehydrated to save
weight.

Potatoes had always been a staple of the German diet,
and the airlift provided them in dehydrated form, a substance called Pom. One girl, recalling the early days of the
airlift, wrote: "The first package of Pom. It was like a
magic show. Will it really turn into something or will it
be all lumpy? Three neighbors watched. They didn't really
dare try it. Mother was more resolute. 'It's getting thick!
Look! It's getting good and thick,' cried Frau Schulze, and
the first dehydrated potato soup with mother's green vegetables cut up in it tasted wonderful to all of us."

Getting the green vegetables that mother combined with
the Pom was an onerous daily chore, no matter how it was
accomplished. Some might be obtained from the eastern
sector. There was no restriction, yet, on travel between the
sectors, and at almost all hours of the day the S-Bahn
(elevated) stations were crowded with men, women, and
children carrying satchels or sacks or boxes to and from the
Russian zone to seek cabbage, lettuce, cauliflower, and
turnips. Others bicycled to the suburbs of the western
sectors, or walked, pulling two or four wheeled carts. In
earlier days the Nazis had proudly introduced the *Volkswagen*— the people's car. These carts were now sarcastically
called *Volkswagen*. And there were gardens. Every minute
of daylight in the early morning and evening was spent
cultivating every available plot of soil in Berlin, or

laboriously transporting dirt for gardens on rooftops or in window boxes. American engineers bulldozed rubble out of the way to expose land for community gardens.

Fuel was of even greater concern than food. The coal flown in by airlift was not available to individuals; it was limited to power plants, bakeries, hospitals, and other special uses. On week ends, Berliners trudged into the suburbs pulling their *Volkswagens* to collect sticks and branches. One correspondent commented on a spry little old man, "he looks about eighty," who trudged past his office every morning pulling his little cart and returned at dusk with a small load of wood.

One might get a *stubbin* permit which entitled the bearer to dig out the stumps of trees that had been destroyed or cut down, but also required him to fill in the holes of three other stumps. Oldsters, women, and children labored long excavating stumps; perhaps ten hours' work digging and refilling holes might produce enough green wood to smolder listlessly for half the time it took to dig it. Others preferred to root in the rubble of bombed houses, digging into cellars in the hope of finding coal buried under the debris or of tearing out the wood of empty coal bins.

Closets, attics, and cellars were combed for long-forgotten oil lamps or lanterns; the British were flying in kerosene in their tankers. After the price of factory-made candles rose out of reach, with virtually none available at any price, experiments were made applying various substances to tightly rolled newspaper in efforts to make torches that would provide light. Some ingenious gadgeteers made hand-operated generators from scrap, that would make a small bulb glow dimly, as long as the cranker's arm held out.

Officially, no clothing was available. Most of the women of the city looked like charwomen going to their daily chores. The black market was the principal source of things to wear, and the supply was limited, not only by the capacity to pay, but by the ability to find anything wearable. Most women wore cotten dresses, patched with parts of old garments. There was some old silk in evidence, virtually no wool. Shoes were a particular problem and most children went barefoot. Adult shoes were sometime entirely homemade of various kinds of ersatz material, soled with straw or wood. Women's stockings practically did not exist except on the black market, where they sold for twelve new marks—about $4. Few women wore hats and men appeared with ancient special purpose headgear—Sunday hats, sporting hats, etc.—which had lain long in closets to be resurrected after the ordinary hats had fallen to pieces.

Stores offered a pathetic assortment of merchandise. One correspondent who went shopping reported that he was able to buy "... pins and pickles; combs and paper bags; rubber heels, shoe laces and wooden buttons; scraps of thread for mending, and kitchen knives, all of the poorest quality—an American dime store would be ashamed to stock them ... On the other hand, there are quantities of flowers—an old woman told me that flowers help you to keep up your courage." This same reporter commented that he could not get his laundry done until he provided soap from the Army Post Exchange, and that he endeared himself to the telegraphers in the press center by permitting them to clean out his ash tray and keep the cigarette butts.

Life was, at best, a semi-primitive existence. Berliners rose early, after being up much of the night to take advantage of the period when the electricity was on. Many walked five or six miles to and from work in the dark. The S-Bahn, whose current was supplied from the Soviet sector, was undependable—sometimes inexplicably stopped for hours. And street cars built to carry 125 passengers were loaded with 175 or more. But those who walked to work were the lucky ones—at least they had jobs. One after another industrial firm closed due to lack of power, and unemployment was on the rise. Women stood for hours in long queues waiting for rations or scrounged for precious articles such as soap, matches, candles, paper to patch shoe soles.

Schools struggled on without light or even textbooks. Many Berlin children had never tasted real candy. Their treat was an ersatz lollypop made without sugar which might last as long as twenty minutes if they sucked very slowly. Radios were heard by pooling to save irreplaceable batteries. There was no glass to replace a broken window, no private transportation except bicycles and no parts to repair them. There was no malt for beer, no typewriter ribbons for offices, no paint, no cosmetics, no hardware, no toys—none of most of the things that Western civilization had long taken for granted. Still, the Berliners quipped; "Rather Pom than *Frau komm*" and, "We'd rather go hungry than go Commie."

The blockade gave rise to a number of new occupations. There was an unofficial post office carried on by boys who, for a tip, would carry a letter from the west sector to the east and mail it there so that it would reach Leipzig or

Dresden quicker and without censorship. The same boys would carry letters or packages from the east to the west sectors that were addressed to destinations in the western zone—Hamburg, Frankfort or Munich.

At every important intersection in West Berlin there were men and women who made their livings exchanging east marks for west marks, and vice versa, at a constantly fluctuating ratio, although the west mark was always worth at least three east marks. Later there would be official exchange bureaus under private ownership. The currency reform, which was supposed to curb the black market, actually seemed to cause a resurgence. For those who had the wherewithal, shoes, food, clothing, tobacco, schnapps, and much else were available from black-market traders— now for west marks rather than cigarettes. Those who could afford it might buy meat in a stationery store, chocolate at the barber's, coal at a drug store, and wool at a coal yard.

There were a few small satisfactions. When the blockade started, a store of 10,000 tons of coal belonging to the Russians was found in the British sector. The English "borrowed" it and blandly gave the Russians a receipt. One who suffered from the blockade was Marshal Sokolovsky. The gas for heating in his posh villa in Potsdam came from the British sector. As soon as this was discovered, somebody gleefully turned it off, and the Russian had to move.

Then, when the Anglo-Americans decided to crack down on the Russian officers who sped through the western sectors to their homes in the suburbs, Sokolovsky was one of the first to be caught in a speed trap. Zooming along at sixty-five mph in a twenty mph zone, his black limousine was stopped by an American traffic patrol of an armored car and a jeep. From a car following Sokolvsky's poured guards brandishing Tommy guns and screaming "Marshal, Marshal," but in true Western style, an American M.P. had the marshal covered. A sergeant called a lieutenant; the lieutenant called a colonel. The colonel called the marshal's attention to the speed limit, and after almost an hour's delay, Sokolovsky drove off at a sedate twenty mph. General Clay later called the Russian to apologize for the inconvenience but no effort was made to chastise the Americans who were responsible for the incident.

Clay's apology was probably sincere for Sokolovsky, as an individual, was well liked. In fact, early in the occupation, one analyst ventured the opinion that the American, French, and British generals on the Allied Control Council probably liked the Russian marshal better than any of them liked each other. Sokolovsky was a military officer rather than a dedicated Communist. His duty required him to execute the orders that he constantly received from Moscow and from commissars like Tulpanov, the propaganda chief. But, personally, he was a mild, well-mannered man whose greatest fault was collaring anyone who would look to show them pictures of his two children. Even after the blockade started, he tried to divorce his social life from his official life and continue to entertain his opposite numbers —and no attempt was made to force liquor on guests at his parties. A Western official, who knew him well, said of him: "He is a man who you would like to have as your friend, and he would be a credit to any country."

As always, the conduct of the Russians was unpredictable. At times they were affable, friendly, and seemed to be the crude, jolly fellows that the Americans had first visioned. The next day, in the same situation, they might be sullen and suspicious, confining their intercourse to the word *nyet*. Typical of their incomprehensible actions was the story of a German girl near the east sector border who went weeping to a Russian M.P. post to complain that a Red Army man had attacked her and stolen her bicycle. The Russians consoled her, wiped her tears, and promised to get back her bicycle. They performed this act of kindness by attacking another girl and taking *her* bicycle away to give to the first girl.

In their attempts to influence or control the Germans, the Soviets still alternated between carrot and stick tactics. On July 19, Moscow issued a decree that all of Berlin would be fed by the Russians. The inhabitants of each west sector borough were directed to register in a designated east sector borough, and they could then buy all the food to which the more liberal eastern ration cards entitled them. Next day the Communist press headlined, "Airlift Has No Purpose—in the Future All Berliners Can Buy Their Rations in the East Sector." The Soviet-dominated newspapers emphasized the quality and quantity of the food available and pointed out that the fresh meats and vegetables in the east sector were far better than the dried and tinned products provided by the airlift. Further, said the Russian propaganda, there was so much coal arriving in East Berlin that there was hardly room to store it.

The result of this highly propagandized offer indicated the extreme distrust of the Germans for Communists. Two weeks after the offer had been made only 19,000 out of 2,000,000 in the west sectors had registered in the Soviet sector. At the ration office in Treptow, in the eastern sector, only 20 people showed up, out of 285,000 who were eligible. At several offices in the borough of Mitte, nobody came to register. One democratic paper editorialized: "Apparently even the Communists from West Berlin don't want to register in the eastern paradise—or else there are so few of them left."

The Soviets continued their harassing tactics on several fronts. General Howley was a victim of a campaign designed to unnerve him. He received strange telephone calls late at night. Sometimes a threatening voice would warn him to get out of Berlin; other times there would be silence when he picked up the receiver. His doorbell also rang at all hours, but there was no one there when the door was opened. To set an example, the American military commander in Berlin refused to surround himself with guards, but the Communist media depicted him as a nervous wreck and periodically announced that his panic-stricken wife had taken the children back to the States. However, Mrs. Howley and their four children calmly stayed in Berlin for the general's entire tour of duty.

More strenuous tactics were used against the democratic leaders of the Berlin government. The Soviets kept them under constant pressure in an effort to completely disorganize the city administration. A favorite tactic was to subject officials to lengthy conferences and interrogations late into the night. One official reported that on the average of once a week he was summoned to Soviet headquarters where he was harangued for hours on end through the night, by a succession of Russian officers, on the necessity for cooperating with the Socialist Unity Party. It was also

common practice for Russians to visit city government offices and remain for hours asking questions and demanding
to see documents. In some cases, they moved desks into
the working quarters of city officials, some of whom were
driven close to a nervous breakdown by the strain of having Soviet personnel constantly peering over their shoul-
ders.

Kidnapping from the western sectors by the MVD and
the Communist-controlled police continued, although
with less frequency since Western M.P.s in machine gun-
bearing jeeps patrolled their section around the clock. Russian M.P.s and eastern police took to grabbing any Western
civilian who inadvertently crossed the line into their zone
to "interrogate" him, a process that frequently took overnight.

East zone police and Russian M.P.s started to intensify
their raids on black-market operators and their customers
in the Potsdamer Platz, the square where the Russian,
British, and American zones met. During three years this
had become almost a game in which a look-out, atop a pile
of rubble, yelled *"razzia"* (raid) when he spotted an abnor-
mal number of policemen. Black-market traders, customers,
and onlookers would then scurry up the streets leading
to the American and British sectors, returning to business
as usual when the police left. Then one day, the pattern
changed. When the familiar cry of *razzia* was raised, the
black marketeers fled as usual, but part of the crowd, estimated as large as 4000, held their ground and started to
pelt the Russians with rubble. When the police retaliated
by firing into the crowd, it fell back into the American
sector. As occupation troops came up from both sides to

restore order, armed Russian and American troops were left facing each other in the center of the square.

During the next few days the Russians staged more raids; during some they pursued their quarry over 100 yards into the American sector, hauling civilians back across the line into their own sector. Until this time, the sector boundaries had been marked only on maps, with some meeting points designated by signs. Now the British and Americans painted broad lines on the pavement of Potsdamer Platz, backed up with metal fences and ranks of M.P.s. These flimsy barricades started the trend that finally culminated in the Berlin wall.

The beginning of the complete political separation of East and West Berlin started in July, 1948, with the establishment of two police forces. The police were still headed by Paul Markgraf, the ex-Nazi officer who had been converted to Communism during his captivity in Russia. Markgraf was completely a tool of the Russians, servile to his masters, arrogant and severe with his subordinates. He also consumed straight schnapps in fabulous quantities. One of his juniors said: "Markgraf is not an ordinary drunk. He is the real discoverer of drink." Except by his masters, Markgraf was universally disliked. It was generally known that he followed Russian orders in connection with kidnappings and other terror tactics. When, during the last two weeks of July, he started a campaign to weed out non-Communists from the higher echelons of the police force by dismissing 590 non-Communist officers, the Magistrat rebelled.

They could not dismiss him without the approval of the occupying authorities, but under the Berlin constitution they could suspend him from duty. This they did and re-placed him with a non-Communist professional policeman, Johannes Stumm, as acting Police President. Kotikov promptly issued an order—signed "Military Commandant of the City of Berlin"—which instructed the city govern-ment to reinstate Markgraf and dismiss Stumm. The West-ern military authorities replied that Kotikov spoke only for the Russians; his order had no validity outside the eastern sector.

Stumm moved his headquarters to the western zone and informed the police force that it was up to the individual to decide whom to obey. This resulted in the bulk of the force moving into the West and gave the city two separate forces; each claimed to have the sole legal authority. From that time on, any western sector police officers who entered the eastern sector were arrested by their Communist-con-trolled brother officers, and several were kidnapped from their own sector, beaten up, and stabbed. Letters posted in East Berlin addressed to the West Berlin police head-quarters were sent to a dead letter office. In one comic opera situation, Markgraf refused to let a new Berlin tele-phone directory be distributed in the eastern sector because it listed Stumm's office under "police headquarters."

The independence of the municipal authorities in the matters of both the currency reform and the police, and the failure of harassing tactics to bring its leaders into line, led the Russians to more active efforts to break down the elected government. On August 26, a Communist rally was held in the east sector at which speakers exhorted the crowd to "frustrate a reactionary plot" and "settle their score with parties in the city government." Spearheaded by truckloads of youthful Communists who had been plied with sausages, cigarettes, and schnapps, a crowd of about 4000 marched to the Stadhaus where a meeting of the Assembly was scheduled for 2 P.M. Word of their coming had preceded them, and the meeting had been called off. Part of the crowd surged into the council chamber, where youngsters in bright sweaters and shorts pretended that they were assemblymen while their leaders harangued them with more speeches. They soon became bored and drifted off.

A *Time* correspondent reported an amusing story that illustrated the meticulous plan behind the "popular uprising" as well as the German pattern of order combined with the Communist demand for obedience. East sector police were present, presumably to protect the building, but they made no effort to restrain the crowd until a few youths surged toward an iron gate. Then one cop stepped in front of them and cried, in outrage, "No, no, not *now*. First you finish singing the *Internationale,* then we let you break down the gate."

The next day a smaller mob returned while the Assembly was in session. For a while, they were kept out by a half-dozen aged civilian employees of the city government, while the east sector police lounged on the sidelines. Then a Soviet officer in the building demanded that he be let out the front door, and part of the crowd surged in as he left, waving Red banners and placards and chanting Communist songs. The meeting was quickly adjourned, and the youths again took over the chamber.

On September 6, the Assembly decided to make another attempt to meet in the Stadhaus. This time forty-six western sector police in civilian clothes volunteered to preserve order in the city hall during the meeting. The much smaller mob which broke down the front door of the building an hour before the meeting was to start consisted almost entirely of trained "action squads" of young German Communists—brawny teen-aged goons spoiling for a fight. Several reporters from West Berlin newspapers, an English journalist, and two American radio reporters were beaten up. The Assembly never had an opportunity to start its business. Most assemblymen sized up the situation and quietly left. Communist leaders then called their own Assembly meeting, with members of the Socialist Unity Party, and established a rump Assembly which quickly voted to put the Socialist Unity Party program into effect.

The Russian terror tactics had succeeded, as they had in Hungary and Czechoslovakia, in destroying an elected government—but Berlin was different. The democratic majority of the Assembly moved into the British sector and called a meeting for that afternoon in the Taberna Academia Building, although there were no desks or chairs in this structure that was normally used for all kinds of festivities. Henceforth, this became the West Berlin City Hall. The split of Berlin was complete with the establishment of two city governments.

Meanwhile, back in the Stadhaus, Markgraf had learned of the presence of the west sector police and sent 200 eastern police, accompanied by some Red Army troops, to surround the building and comb it for the western police. Twenty of them took refuge in the office of the American liaison officer and the remainder in the British and French offices. The Russians forced their way into the American office, held a lieutenant at bay with a Tommy gun, and dragged out the twenty western police who had sought American protection. Those who had taken refuge in the British and French offices were, for a time, more fortunate. The Markgraf police and Red Army troops drew a ring around the building and demanded that the Stumm police be turned over to them, but made no effort to take them. Next morning the French commandant, General Koenig, obtained a promise from Marshal Sokolovsky that the men could leave the building unharmed. This he passed to General Kotikov, who agreed to honor it. Forty hours after the "siege within a siege" had started, the French sent two trucks to pick up the remaining western sector police, relying on Sokolovsky's and Kotikov's safe conduct. The weary, frightened men filed out in the predawn dark and climbed into the trucks. Four blocks away two Soviet jeeps, bristling with machine guns, brought them to a halt. Seventy-five eastern police swarmed from the shadows of a nearby building and cuffed their western colleagues out of the trucks and off to a Soviet sector prison.

The attacks on the city government, and the arrest of the western police, caused a wave of rage to sweep West Berlin. Three days later, on September 9, a protest meeting was called in Platz der Republik, a huge square flanked on one side by the gutted Reichstag building and, on another, by the towering memorial Brandenburg Gate which marked the boundary between the British and Russian sections. Three hundred thousand outraged Berliners jammed the square—the greatest voluntary mass meeting in German history. Even Hitler had never commanded such a crowd in Berlin. *Time*'s bureau chief cabled that

there was enough mass power in the Berlin throng to
change the fate of Europe.

The 300,000 blanketed the whole rubble-strewn area before the Reichstag, and choked every path through the
Tiergarten. They stood quietly under the hot sun in or-
derly ranks between rows of cabbages in the little garden
plots and listened to a Social Democrat leader proclaim,
"He who surrenders Berlin surrenders the world, surrenders himself." They cheered a labor leader who bel-
lowed, "The blockade has failed, and now the Communists
can only wait for the help of General Hunger and General-
issimo Winter. Again they will fail."

While the speaking continued, the crowd was well be-
haved, confining itself to shouted approval of each speaker's
condemnation of the Russians. Unlike Soviet-inspired demonstrations, there were no action squads to take the lead
in violence. What happened next was spontaneous and
unplanned. As the crowd broke up, trouble flared in one
spot, subsided, then flared again blocks away over a period
of two hours. First, thousands who poured through the
Brandenburg Gate on their way to homes in the eastern
sector passed a Soviet truck on Unter der Linden carrying
a dozen eastern police. The crowd jeered, then a rock was
thrown, then a barrage of bricks and stones flew from the
ruins of the old U.S. Embassy driving the police back and
pelting every Soviet car in sight. When police reinforce-
ments arrived, firing pistols in the air, the crowd fell back
through the arches of the Brandenburg Gate to join the
throng that had remained in the square. The mob was unusual in that it seemed to combine resolution with timid-
ity. One group that halted a Soviet car beat a hasty re-

treat when a Russian officer stepped from it, stamped his foot on the pavement, and shook his fist.

When the mob again surged forward toward the gate, reinforced police and Soviet troops fired into and over them. Most of the Germans hit the ground but one fifteen-year-old boy who dropped too late received a fatal bullet in the stomach. While this was happening the Russians were too busy to note four or five boys who were climbing the Doric columns of the Brandenburg Gate. High above the square one youth shinnied up the flagpole atop the gate, tore the Red flag from its halyard, and threw it down to the crowd. While some struggled to tear pieces off the flag for souvenirs, the rest of the throng raised the cry *aufbrennen* (burn it). Before this could be done a jeep-load of Soviet soldiers roared up to the gate, firing their Tommy guns in the air. When a squad of British M.P.s took up positions between the crowd and their Russian adversaries, the latter held their fire, and the former slowly dispersed.

As riots go, the trouble at the Brandenburg Gate was relatively mild, with one killed and twenty-three injured, mostly by thrown stones. One reporter commented on the commendable restraint of the Soviet police, and troops in general, by withholding their fire. It is more likely that the Russian restraint was due to surprise rather than consideration for the Germans. The turn of the worm was totally un-expected, and the Russian troops and their puppet police had no orders to cope with it. Also, this was another in-stance that, when faced with determined opposition, the Russians backed down. Although they had ten times the armed force of the Western powers in and around Berlin, they did not want a shooting affray.

The Brandenburg Gate riot was significant because it marked the end of the summer of indecision. More than ten percent of the population of West Germany had gathered before the Reichstag to forcefully express their defiance of the Russians—of whom, a few short months before, they had lived in deadly fear. They still feared the Russians, but as the summer ended, confidence was becoming stronger, and righteous anger had surmounted fear. The credit for this change might be given equally to the staunch leadership of the democratic parties—and to the airlift. For it was the latter that gave assurance to most Berliners that they were not alone in their fight for freedom. So long as the airplane engines droned continuously overhead, they knew that they had the backing of the British and the Americans.

Recalling the airlift that summer, one unskilled worker later wrote, "Early in the morning, when we woke up, the first thing we did was listen to see whether the noise of aircraft engines could be heard. That gave us the certainty that we were not alone, that the whole civilized world took part in the fight for Berlin's freedom."

Another presented the matter more graphically in this description of the feelings of the people when, at night, the noise of the engines suddenly ceased. "Suddenly, outside the windows and above the roofs, there is a paralyzing silence. It weighs on one like the silence of a corpse. All at once a whole city is listening to stillness, and in the breasts of hundreds of thousands, terrible uncertainty begins to arise. The airlift has stopped. What has happened? Are they going to abandon us? Will we have to submit? It seems that all life is suspended for several minutes. Then—

after an eternity—the roar can be heard again, and there are a hundred thousand sighs of relief."

At first, those who lived near airports could not sleep because of the noise of the engines. Later, many reported that they woke with a feeling of unease whenever the planes did not maintain their steady patterns of arrivals. One who reported this experience was General Clay, whose residence was directly under the approach to Templehof.

The confidence that the summer had brought was not so strong as to the future. Winter would bring a need for additional tonnage of coal, the most difficult commodity to fly in. More important, winter weather would surely curtail flights. In a public opinion survey only 45 percent of the people questioned thought that the airlift could bring in enough supplies to carry Berlin through the winter—52 percent thought that it could not, and the rest had no opinion. But many thought, or hoped, that the blockade would not continue through the winter. If it did—well, that was something to face when the time came.

In anticipation of the greater hardships to come, the RAF inaugurated Operation Stork to fly out children to foster homes in West Germany. During the war, they had evacuated their own kids from bomb-threatened London, sending trainloads to farms and villages in the country and shiploads to Canada. Now they flew over 15,000 German kids to new homes where there was warmth, light, and fresh milk.

Every morning fathers and mothers appeared at Gatow with their offspring to turn them over to the RAF. As long lines of youngsters trooped aboard the planes there were few dry eyes at the airport—except for the children themselves who were, on the whole, braver than the parents. They reminded one reporter of soldiers on their way to the front, scared but too proud to show it. Berliners were somewhat cheered by letters that came back to the beleaguered city, such as this that was published in a West Berlin paper:

"Dear Mummy: When we were taking off you looked smaller and smaller and then I could no longer see you. We flew above the clouds quite high in the sky. I wish we would have remained in the air for a year it was so wonderful. Every morning I have milk and eggs which I am allowed to get for myself in the henhouse. I already know all of the cows and pigs, one of whom is called Lottchen. When I come back you will not know me anymore because I am getting so big and strong."

FIVE

The Undramatic Ton-Mile

It was Friday, August 13, 1948. It was raining in Berlin. This was not unusual, but this day's deluge was not an ordinary rain storm. Through the torrential downpour the tower controllers could not see the runway, and radar, which could penetrate clouds, fog, or darkness, was virtually useless in heavy rain.

When the morning string of planes took off from Rein-Main conditions were not too bad. The cloud cover lowered as they crossed the spur of the Harz Mountains that jutted into the corridor. By the time the leading plane neared Templehof the clouds were hugging the roof of the apartment house at the edge of the field, pouring down an almost impenetrable curtain of rain. The first C-54 overshot the runway, crashed into a ditch, and burst into flames. The crew got out safely. The pilot of the second plane landed too far down the runway and, in an effort to avoid the flaming plane ahead, braked so hard that he blew both tires. Another pilot, coming in low over the housetops, saw what he thought was a runway and landed on what proved to be an auxiliary strip that was under construction.

In desperation, the harassed controllers in the tower started to stack the remaining planes. This is a normal operation in commercial aviation when landings must be deferred. Each plane circles continuously at a prescribed altitude, one plane above another. In commercial flying, this is done in a prearranged area fifty to one hundred miles away from the field, where the planes can fly their monotonous circles in the great open spaces. At Berlin it had to be done in a twenty-mile circle over the city; if the planes ranged wider they would be over Russian territory where they might be subject to Soviet attack. To further confuse the situation, a traffic jam was developing on the ground where unloaded planes were piling up, unable to take off for fear of colliding with the circling planes above.

In the service vernacular, it was a grand SNAFU. Twenty-five or more planes were circling at altitudes of from three to fifteen thousand feet, their pilots adding to the hubbub by chattering over the radio to find out what was happening. Suddenly, through the chatter, a stern voice sounded loud and clear, "This is 5549, Tunner talking; and you listen. Send every plane in the stack back to its home base."

After a moment of dead silence an incredulous voice from the tower said, "Please repeat."

"Send everybody in the stack above and below me home. Then tell me when it's O.K. to come down."

"Roger, sir," replied the tower and proceeded to issue orders that sent the milling planes streaking down the center corridor to Rein-Main with their loads of coal.

The voice of command was that of Major General (now Lieutenant General) William H. Tunner who had taken command of the airlift fifteen days before its Black Friday dawned. The foul-up was particularly embarrassing to

Tunner on that day because of the nature of his errand to Berlin. A few days before, an old German had come to headquarters at Wiesbaden with a present that he wanted to give to the airlift. The gift was a magnificent gold, jewel-studded hunting watch in a velvet case, which had originally belonged to the old man's great-grandfather. It was probably worth over $5000, and it was the only thing of value the donor owned. But he insisted that he wanted to give it to the men who were saving his beloved Berlin, "as a little token from an old and grateful heart."

Under the circumstances Tunner could not refuse the old man's offer and told him that he would present it to the pilot who had made the most airlift flights, in a public ceremony at Templehof. The pilot was located—Lieutenant Paul O. Lykins—and told to stand by on August 13, in his best uniform. A speaker's platform was built; a band and a guard of honor were waiting to take their places on the field. Tunner was on his way to make the presentation in a ceremony which, incidentally, honored the smooth-running efficiency of the airlift, when his plane was stacked at 8000 feet. As he later wrote, "We expected thousands of people, and here I was circling over their heads. It was damned embarrassing. The commander of the Berlin Airlift couldn't even get himself to Berlin."

In 1948 General Tunner was the country's—nay, the world's—leading authority on airlifting. Although he was a pilot, most of his assignments in the Air Corps after his first years out of West Point were tactical ones, involving mainly administrative duties. In the spring of 1941, as a major, he was the third officer assigned to the newly created Ferrying Command, which he later headed when it became part of the Air Transport Command. Up to that time there had been no transport service in the Air Corps; there had, in fact, been no transport planes. Tunner pioneered a new aspect of military aviation.

The Ferrying Command was created to deliver tens of thousands of airplanes from the factories in which they were built to the point at which they could be used for combat—an operation which Tunner soon realized required entirely different systems, methods, and even personnel from combat flying. The combat pilot was supposed to do whatever was necessary to inflict damage on the enemy. If, in the process, he took risks that resulted in the loss of his plane, this was to be expected and the pilot might be regarded as a hero. A pilot who was cautious, or conservative, or sparing of his ship was not a good combat pilot. In the Ferrying Command, exactly the reverse was true. Ferry pilots were not supposed to take chances that involved risks to pilot or plane. Their job was to fly skillfully and safely so as to deliver the plane in good condition and be available to take out another one. Although the pilots who pioneered transoceanic delivery routes ran great risks, the Air Transport Command fliers were belittled by their combat brethren, who said that ATC stood for "Allergic to Combat," or "Army of Terrified Civilians."

One of Tunner's pioneering feats was the use of female ferry pilots. In his memoirs, he intimates that they were, on the whole, better than men for this type of flying, in that they were more amenable to flying by the book and had less cowboy propensities. In any event, the women had a better safety record than the men.

In the Ferrying Command, Tunner developed a highly

professional staff of officers devoted exclusively to air transport. This was a new concept in the Air Corps. Previously, any transport activities had been casually delegated to some subordinate officer by a combat commander. Wrote Tunner: "Though great in their own field—combat—these commanders cared little and thought less about transport; to them it was something anybody could do."

When the history of the Air Transport Command was written, the official historian described Tunner as, "An unusually handsome man, cold in his manner except with a few intimates, somewhat arrogant, brilliant, competent. . . . His loyalty to the organization he commanded was notable and so was his ability to maintain the loyalty of his men. The men of his Division held themselves to be somewhat apart from the rest of the Command; even after he had been transferred to India and many of them were scattered into other parts of the organization, they remained Tunner's men. . . . Air Transport Command headquarters came to look upon him with a mixture of exasperation, admiration, and reliance. They wished he would mend his ways, be less independent, more willing to conform. Action to realize this wish was baffled by the frequency with which the nonconformist proved to be in the right."

In August 1944, Tunner was assigned to command the Hump Airlift, with headquarters in Upper Assem, India. Immediately upon arrival, he piloted the first plane that was ready over the mountains to China, had a meal of fresh eggs, and flew back. He then took the slip that he received from the debriefing officer to the dispensary and got two ounces of whisky. These were the special rewards for flying over the world's highest and most rugged mountains: *Flied Eggis,* as the Chinese waiters called them, at one end and a drink of bonded Old Crow at the other.

Tunner was given a two pronged assignment when he took command of the Hump Airlift: to increase tonnage and to decrease the appalling accident rate. The tonnage for the month before he took over was 22,000 tons. A year later in the last big month, July 1945, supplies flown to China totaled 71,042 tons. Accidents in early 1944 were at the rate of 2 per 1000 flying hours. A year later the rate was 2 per 8000 flying hours. Tunner did it, said the official history of the Army Air Forces, by introducing "the age of big business" to military flying.

When the Berlin Airlift started Tunner was back in Washington. A few months previously the Military Air Transport Service—MATS—had been created by combining the Air Transport Command with a few squadrons of the Naval Air Transport Service. Tunner was Deputy Commander for Operations of MATS. His initial proposal to his superior that MATS take over the airlift, made a few days after the lift started, was ignored until General Wedemeyer again entered the picture. In Berlin, Wedemeyer had suggested the airlift to Clay. Now he sent a confidential memorandum to General Hoyt Vandenberg, Chief of Staff of the Air Force. As the commanding general in China, Wedemeyer had been on the receiving end of the Hump Airlift and knew what Tunner had done. He recommended to Vandenberg that Tunner be placed in command of the Berlin Airlift. The appointment was made, but when Tunner left for Germany he knew that there were three people there who did not approve it:

Generals Clay, LeMay, and Smith. After all they had a good thing going; it was working—quite well, they thought —and it was making headlines all around the globe. Why should a strange, hot-shot specialist be brought in to take over?

Although he gave great credit to LeMay and Smith for a magnificent job in getting the airlift started, Tunner, while still in Washington, did not feel that it was running well— or as well as it could. He wrote, "To any of us familiar with the airlift business, some of the features of Operation Vittles which were most enthusiastically reported in the press were contradictions of efficient administration. Pilots were flying twice as many hours per week as they should, for example; newspaper stories told how they continued on, though exhausted. I read how desk officers took off whenever they got the chance and ran to the flight line to find planes sitting there waiting for them. This was all very exciting, and loads of fun, but successful operations are not built on such methods. . . . The actual operation of a successful airlift is about as glamorous as drops of water on a stone. There's no frenzy, no flap, just the inexorable process of getting the job done. . . . The real excitement from running a successful airlift comes from seeing a dozen lines climbing steadily on a chart—tonnage delivered, utilization of aircraft, and so on—and the lines representing accidents and injuries going sharply down. That's where the glamor lies in air transport."

When Tunner arrived in Germany at the end of July 1948, he found, as he expected, what he termed a "cowboy operation." Everything was hustle and bustle. Some of the "off we go into the wild blue yonder" spirit still

prevailed, although many of the fliers were already getting heartily sick of the operation. Much was made in
the press of the daring and excitement of the life-saving
flights to Berlin, but one English writer who stayed around
somewhat longer than most of the reporters commented on
"the soul-destroying monotony of the routine. The aircraft was a cog in a great machine. . . . The barracks were
a seething, dead-weary dormitory in which there was no
night and no day, only constant getting up and feeding and
going to bed of men who ticked off hours flown on their
schedule sheets like boys marking off the days to the end
of the term."

The new commander immediately started to make some
changes. One of the first, put into effect only three days
after he arrived, led the fliers to believe that his behind-
the-back-nickname from the Hump days—"Willie the
Whip"—was well justified. On his first inspection trip to
Berlin. Tunner noted that there was much milling around
of flight personnel. Crews left their planes while they were
being unloaded to smoke, lounge, and gossip in a snack
bar. When the planes were ready to take off on their return trips the crews frequently were not. Tunner ordered
that henceforth crews were not to leave their planes at
Tempelhof. Each plane would be met by two jeeps, one
with an operations officer and the other with a weather man
to tell the pilot anything he needed to know for his return
trip. A third vehicle, a Volkswagen van equipped as a
snack bar, would come to the plane to provide for the inner
man. The flier's initial resentment at this restriction vanished when they found that Tunner had asked the German
Red Cross to staff the snack van with their prettiest *Fräu-*

leins to dispense charm with the goodies. From that time on, you could not chase the crews away from the planes—and turn-around time was brought down to thirty minutes flat.

Another thing that Tunner found that was surprising in view of the stories that were appearing in the home press was that morale was low, even in August, and getting worse. Many of the airlift personnel did not appreciate the importance of the airlift in terms of the foreign policy of their country or the fate of a free Europe. Others were essentially combat men who, after the first few exciting weeks, were finding this a monotonous and irksome job. And there were some who simply could not understand why, after fighting the Germans for almost four years, they were now breaking their backs feeding them. One pilot was quoted as saying: "What I try to do now is fly one flight a day instead of two. That way I beat those bastards in Berlin out of 10,000 tons of coal." Another expressed an attitude that was typical of at least a minority of the group when he said: "I've had enough. I want to go home. I've got enough problems of my own without worrying about the ones the gooney birds have. They asked for it, didn't they?" (The reference to gooney birds here is to Germans, not to C-47s.)

But the principal cause for low morale was that most airlift personnel were on temporary assignment from some other base, whereas occupation force and USAFE personnel were permanently assigned to Germany. This meant that the latter, many of whom had brought their families over, had permanent quarters in the best housing available, while the airlift personnel slept in crowded barracks;

and with the constant coming and going of crew members at all hours that the schedule involved, it was frequently hard to sleep. Rein-Main was at 150 percent capacity with more people pouring in every day; it had the worst living conditions of any American air base in the world. Indicative of the double standard for the occupation forces and the airlift was that General LeMay was quartered in a fifty-five room mansion that had been requisitioned from a German industrialist, maintained by a staff of fifteen servants, while General Tunner was quartered in one room on the third floor of a walk-up hotel, which could only be entered through a bathroom.

As their temporary assignments were extended again and again, many of the men became resentful at being separated from their families. The troop-carrying group that had come from Hickam Field had been stationed in Hawaii only a few weeks when the order came assigning them to Germany for temporary duty. Their wives and children were aboard a ship coming from San Francisco to Hawaii when the group flew over their heads going in the other direction en route to Germany. Wives arrived in Honolulu three days later to find that their husbands had left and did not know when their men would return. This situation was not unique to the Hawaiian group, and when wives and sweethearts around the world received word that the absence of their men had been indefinitely extended, "Dear John" letters started to arrive in Germany. This situation was aggravated, for a few of the men, by a poison-pen letter campaign initiated by the Russians. Mysterious, anonymous letters were received by the pilots reporting the infidelity of wives or sweethearts.

The most common complaint of the men who were represented in the press as being dedicated to saving Berlin from starvation was, "I want to go home." There was little that Tunner could do about the conditions that caused this—he was on temporary duty himself. He fought for and got some private buildings requisitioned to improve the housing situation and demanded a step up in the quality of food. And he detailed Lieutenant Bill Thompson, a Public Relations Officer, to start a newspaper, the *Task Force Times,* an important feature of which was a daily cartoon which satirized USAFE, and cynically but humorously portrayed everything disagreeable that the heroes of the airlift had to put up with.

Principal purpose of the *Task Force Times* was to take the men's minds off their troubles by instilling a spirit of competition in relation to the tonnage transported by each group. The chief topic of conversation on every base became the daily tonnage record. One correspondent told of entering an operations room where an officer was shouting angrily into the phone. He asked a sergeant: "What's he yelling about?"

"Figures," replied the sergeant. "Everybody's tonnage-whacky. He's claiming the tonnage high for the day. Somebody in Wiesbaden gave it to the 313th or some other group. You'd think this was the Kentucky Derby."

Getting permission to publish the figures involved another fight with security officers at USAFE. This, they said, was confidential information. We must not let the Russians know what we are doing. Obviously, Russians had both Gatow and Templehof under constant observation. It was impossible to bring a plane with a ten-ton load in secretly. The Soviets could count, and they could multiply the number of flights by ten to get the total daily tonnage. The security officers finally backed down, but not willingly.

The first weeks of this phase of the airlift were marked by a series of lengthy staff meetings. It was immediately obvious that the obstacles in the way of more efficient operation were on the ground, not in the air. There was still a shortage of every type of ground personnel—weathermen, cooks, mechanics, engineers, radiomen, radarmen, office personnel, doctors, carpenters, drivers. The Air Installations officer reported that both Rein-Main and Wiesbaden were inadequate in length of runways, taxiways, hardstands, fueling facilities, loading and unloading facilities, hangar space, administration buildings, and all lighting—floodlights, approach lights, and hangar lights were all below standard. Communications told Tunner that most existing equipment was obsolete. Beacons and ranges to and from Berlin could not control precision flying in the narrow corridors. There was no ground-control approach system to "talk down" pilots in bad weather. Ground transportation needed more and larger trucks and trailers, spare parts, garages, mechanics, drivers. More roads and storage facilities were an urgent necessity, as were additional railroad spurs. Much of the cargo was improperly packaged, improperly weighed, and improperly tied down. Logistics and maintenance officers added the final problems. The planes were covered with dangerous coal dust which was wrecking delicate instruments. They were not designed to make numerous takeoffs and landings with heavy loads that placed unmerciful stress on engines, brakes, and springs. There were no proper facilities for maintenance, and the spare parts situation was beyond desperation. This was the situation that Tunner and the staff of air transport specialists that he brought with him inherited.

One long staff meeting ended in a laugh when a young lieutenant had a bright idea for solving the shortage in office personnel. "Why not," he asked, "have the Red Cross or somebody send us over a couple of hundred American girls?" To which an engineering officer seriously replied: "We don't have enough housing as it is. Where would they sleep?" Everyone in the room had an answer for this, and the answers were all the same.

The solution of all the individual problems would add up to one major objective—greater plane utilization. This was the answer to a successful airlift, the creation of more ton miles per plane. It was obvious that if there were only so many planes to carry cargo, and each plane could carry only so much cargo on a trip, the only way to increase total tonnage was to have each plane make more trips—to increase plane utilization. It might be said that Tunner hated an airplane on the ground, where it was a worthless hunk of metal.

The Air Force's normal peacetime utilization rate for C-54s was sometimes as low as three and a half hours a day. In the early weeks of the airlift, this was increased to nearly six hours, partly by skimping on maintenance time. Reference was made to planes that were held together by baling wire, and one plane flew for three days without a door. During this later phase of the airlift, plane utilization was increased to nine hours per day, without skimping on maintenance and in all kinds of weather. Because of the unusual nature of the operation, with a short trip in the air bracketed by takeoff and landing, loading and unloading, refueling, briefing and debriefing, this was comparable to a utilization rate of between thirteen and fourteen hours a day on an ocean route or other long-haul use.

The principal factor in plane utilization was maintenance. In addition to a daily preflight inspection for each plane, special, more complete, checks at every fifty hours of flying time, and incidental repairs during routine operations, the planes required a complete overhaul after every 200 hours of flight and a thorough inspection and rebuilding after each 1000 hours; the last a fifteen-day factory operation. Incidental repairs in Berlin were facilitated by the creation of "alert crews" of specialists ready to meet each plane as it landed to take care of any pilot's squawks that had been communicated by radio. The alert crew jeeped to the plane as it landed with special personnel and tools to take care of minor troubles that had been reported from the air. If the pilot had reported propeller trouble, there was a prop man in the jeep; if he squawked about carburetor trouble, there was a fuel systems expert; if the trouble was brakes, there was a hydraulics man. By this system most minor troubles could be fixed within the normal turn-around time.

There was a simple solution to the shortage of mechanics. Many good airplane mechanics were available, but they were Germans, and the "no fraternization" edict that forbade the use of Germans for anything but menial labor was still in effect. Only General Clay could broaden this ruling to permit the use of Germans as mechanics, and regulations forbid Tunner to communicate with Clay except through USAFE headquarters. Fortunately he met the military commander by chance at Templehof one day, and Clay asked him if he had any troubles. When Tunner described the shortage of maintenance men, which could be solved by the use of German mechanics, Clay gave his consent. The first German hired to head up German maintenance personnel was of equal rank to Tunner, ex-*Luftwaffe* Major General Hans von Rohden, who was able to call back scores of crack *Luftwaffe* mechanics. American service manuals were quickly translated into German, a language school was set up, and German speaking supervisors were put with the new men until they learned enough English to carry on. Ultimately, the airlift had more German mechanics than American.

Maintenance had been carried on in a rather helter-skelter manner, with undermanned squadron crews trying to do everything up to the thousand-hour overhaul. As a result of this, and parts shortages, one-third of the planes were sometimes grounded, and planes might sit on the ground for days if a particular part was unobtainable. The first step in relieving this was to reopen an old *Luftwaffe* repair base with the jaw-breaking name of Oberpfaffenhofen—familiarly known as "Oberhuffin-puffin" or simply as "Obie." Here the German mechanics proved invaluable —they could at least pronounce the name of the place. Obie was soon doing a steady seven 200-hour overhauls a day.

For the thousand-hour rebuilding the planes were flown back to the United States and serviced in private factories or at Navy or Air Force bases. It was, by this time, apparent that the airlift, to be successful, must start in the United States rather than Rein-Main. The facilities of MATS and a special naval task force called Marine X were organized to provide a flow of tools, spare parts, and reconditioned engines. Engines were taking a terrible beating under the unusual short-haul conditions of the lift, and at one time it was kept going only by the timely arrival of 100 engines from the Navy, some of which were flown in by MATS and the balance delivered by Marine X.

As plane utilization steadily increased and more C-54s arrived in Germany, a renewed shortage of flight crews loomed. Pilots who had checked out on heavy combat planes were not qualified for this type of work without further instruction, and there were not enough of them in the regular Air Force to meet the three crews per plane requirement of the airlift. Fliers and flight engineers had to be called up from the reserves, and many of them had not flown in three years. So a "Little Airlift" was set up at the Air Force base in Great Falls, Montana, to train crews for the big airlift.

An exact duplicate of the approach to Templehof was established at Great Falls; even the magnetic course for coming in the field was the same as that of Templehof, and the weather was very similar. In C-54s carrying ten tons of sand, three-man crews practiced exactly the same techniques that were required to bring a plane into the Berlin airport, except that every landing was a GCA landing, regardless of the weather. When the new crews trained at Great Falls arrived in Germany they had a feeling that this type of thing was routine flying—they had been doing it all day, every day, for three weeks. At its peak, the Little Airlift turned out twenty-nine crews a week for the big airlift, an addition that finally made it possible to rotate the men who had long been on temporary duty.

Bomb damage in Berlin, August 29, 1945.   U.S. Army Photo

A truckload of black-marketeers arrive at a working place in Berlin to clear up rubble as punishment under the law.   U.S. Army Photo

Hitler's Chancellery viewed from the bombed ruins of the Propaganda Ministry, with the famous balcony shown barricaded in lower center.

Anti-Communist rally in Berlin, September, 1948. U.S. Air Force Photo

Navy pilot Lt. G. W. Bailey of Grafton, N.D., checks a cargo of flour to see that it is properly secured before the plane takes off for Berlin.

U.S. Army Photo

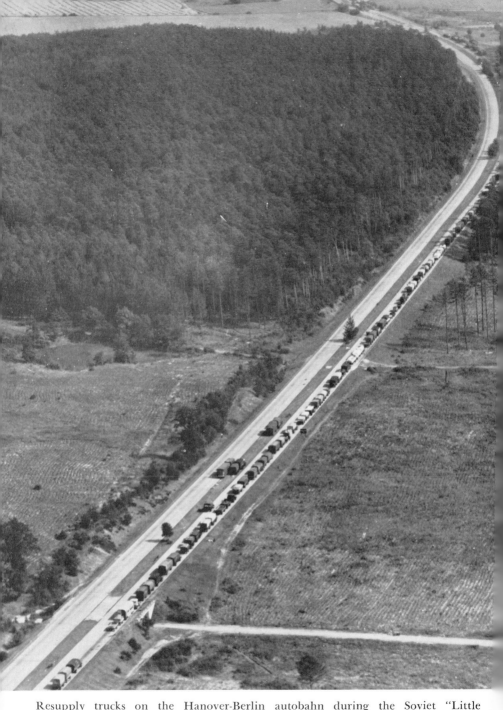

Resupply trucks on the Hanover-Berlin autobahn during the Soviet "Little Blockade." Only four trucks per hour were allowed through the check point at Helmstedt for several days.

U.S. Air Force Photo

A British Army enlisted man directs the parking of a coal truck as German laborers prepare to load an Air Force C-54 at Fassberg Airfield.

View taken from an Operation Vittles plane on the final approach to Tempelhof Airdrome in Berlin.

U.S. Air Force Photo

U.S. Air Force C-54s lined up awaiting take-off from Rhein-Main Air Base at Frankfurt for Berlin.

U.S. Air Force Photo

German youngsters pause in their playing to watch a Douglas C-54 taking off on another mission during Operation Vittles.

High-intensity approach lights illuminate a 3,000-foot approach to the main runway at Tempelhof Airdrome. The 200,000-watt system was designed to assist the landing of USAF planes on Operation Vittles during periods of poor visibility.

Crews unload 25 tons of flour through the lower elevator of a giant Douglas C-74 Globemaster at Tempelhof Airdrome.

A group of C-47
transport planes
in the unloading
line at Tempelhof
Airdrome during
Operation Vittles.

U.S. Air Force Photo

A British Sunderland flying boat unloads 140 cases of egg powder on Lake Wansee in Berlin for the blockaded city.

U.S. Army Photo

First Lt. Gail S. Halvorsen of Garland, Utah, and 17th Military Air Transport Squadron, rigs up candy bars to miniature parachutes for German children in Berlin.

U.S. Air Force Photo

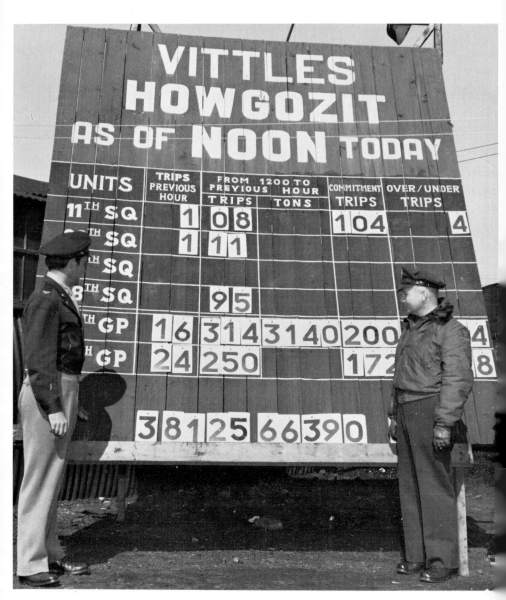

Col. Theron C. Coulter (left) C.O., 60th Troop Carrier Wing and Lt. Col. Conway S. Hall, C.O., 313th Troop Carrier Group (2nd from left), viewing the "HOW-GOZIT" board at Fassberg RAF station which keeps personnel informed about number of flights and tonnage flown to Berlin.

Linda Raspe, from Berlin's west sector, totes her family's weekly bread ration from a bakery. The bread was baked from American Airlift flour and is wrapped in a Soviet-licensed newspaper that carries a banner headline reading: AIRLIFT USELESS.

U.S. Air Force Photo

A little German girl holds one of the thousands of candy bars attached to miniature parachutes which Airlift pilots flying Operation Little Vittles dropped into the blockaded city.

U.S. Air Force Photo

Berlin youngsters living near Tempelhof Air Force Base play a game called "Luftbrücke" (air bridge), using model American planes.

View of maintenance dock area at Oberpfaffenhofen Air Force Depot. These docks were built to facilitate the 200-hour inspection of C-54s engaged in the Berlin Airlift.

A part of the engine "build-up" line at Rhein-Main Air Force Base where engines used on C-54 Skymasters were dis - assembled, checked, worn parts replaced, reassembled and returned to service on the aircraft.

Mounted on a truck, a jet engine from an F-80 Shooting Star is used to melt ice and snow from the wings of C-54s at Tempelhof Air Force Base.

First Lt. Lee Masav of Tempelhof Air Force Base paints the new daily tonnage record of 12,940 tons on a C-54 plane. The date was April 16, 1949.

Airmen of Navy Squadron VR-6 at Rhein-Main Air Force Base in Frankfurt greet a crew as it returned from delivering ten tons of supplies to Tempelhof when the end of the Berlin Blockade became an actuality.

As the airlift was stepped up, there were a few changes in flight procedure. The purpose was to keep up a never-ending beat of planes landing at three-minute intervals around the clock. This was sometimes interrupted by the vagaries of weather at opposite ends of the run. A pilot might take off in bright sunlight in Rein-Main, flying by visual rules. Suddenly he would find himself in a dense cloud cover over the Harz Mountains and have to shift to instrument flying, since he could not change his altitude to avoid the weather. This switching from visual to instrument flying was confusing and perhaps dangerous. Since pilots could fly by instruments in clear weather, but could not fly by sight in foul weather, it was ruled that all flights were to be made on instruments, good weather or bad, night or day.

Another change in procedure resulted from the Black Friday interlude. It was ruled that if a pilot missed his landing on the first approach, for any reason whatsoever, he was to turn into the center corridor and return to home base with his load. Tunner threatened to reduce any pilot to copilot status who *did not* land with ceiling and visibility *greater* than 400 feet and a mile and to court martial any pilot who *did* land with ceiling and visibility of *less than* 400 feet and a mile. He never did reduce or court martial anybody; but the peasants got the point, and when a pilot found a ceiling of less than 400 feet at Templehof, he shoved forward his throttles and streaked for the center corridor, perhaps with a sigh of regret for missing the pretty Red Cross girl on the snack van.

This procedure sometimes caused some strange flights when the returning pilot found Rein-Main and Wiesbaden socked in and had to fly on to an alternate base—Vienna or even Marseilles—with a load of coal for Berlin. The most exciting flight of this nature was one in which the pilot, for some reason that was never determined, took the wrong heading over the Fulda Range. He flew on and on, far longer than the distance to Berlin would require. Finally, through a rift in the clouds, he spotted an airport. By this time he was not choosy as to where he landed. The last gallons of gas were sloshing in his tanks, and he had to come down. He found himself, with crew, plane, and ten tons of coal, in Prague, Czechoslovakia, well behind the Iron Curtain.

Czech Air Force officers at the field greeted these unexpected guests with delight and insisted that they stay for dinner and a party. The Americans were quite willing, but wisely called the American Embassy to announce their arrival. The party had scarcely started when the American military attaché from the embassy arrived at the field and tried to break it up.

"I don't want to seem inhospitable," he said, "but if I were you fellows I'd get the hell out of here as soon as I could. This place is crawling with Russians. The Czechs don't like them any better than we do, but it's the Russians who are calling the shots."

"We're dead tired," said the pilot. "These fellows have offered to put us up for the night. Suppose we get some sleep and take off bright and early in the morning?"

"Well, it's your funeral," said the attaché, "but if anything happens, don't say I didn't warn you."

The party continued joyously, and the Americans finally turned in. They had hardly closed their eyes when they were shaken awake by the military attaché. "The Russians have found out you're here," he said, "and they're looking for you. You'd better get out of here fast."

Dragging on their uniforms the crew dived for the plane, which the Czechs had gassed, and took off in the night. The weather was still bad, but they managed to find their way home. Some time later the military attaché from Prague passed through Wiesbaden. "Every Czech officer who was at that party," he said, "or who had anything to do with you has disappeared—vanished without a trace."

The foul weather procedure was modified when GCA equipment—Ground Control Approach—became available at Berlin in mid-September. The investigation of the SNAFU on Black Friday disclosed that the traffic control operators in the Templehof tower were not experienced in handling anything like the density of airlift traffic. A traffic flow of this type was more typical of a busy civilian commercial airport than of a military base. Tunner got on the phone to MATS, and within four days twenty air reservists who had been working as traffic controllers for the Civil Aeronautics Authority at civilian airports in the United States were back in uniform in Germany.

MATS also flew in, disassembled, two CPN-4 vans— 50,000 pounds of cathode ray tubes, radar, and other delicate electronic devices that represented the very latest in ground control approach equipment which would cut the ceiling and visibility requirements to 300 feet and a quarter of a mile. One of the most spectacular accomplishments of the airlift—to airmen—was its development of GCA landing techniques. This system was used in civil aviation, but a GCA landing at a commercial airport usually involved stacking other planes while fifteen or twenty minutes were spent bringing a plane in. The procedure was so improved on the airlift that GCA landings were made on the planes' regular three-minute headway. By the fall of 1948, on a day of bad weather in Berlin, more GCA landings were made at Templehof than at all the airports in the United States combined.

In flying procedure, GCA took effect when the tower controller had brought the plane down to an altitude of 2000 on its approach to Templehof. At this point, if visual landing requirements were below the minimum, the tower operator would say:

"Baker Easy 34 this is Templehof Airways. You are cleared to Jigsaw. Contact Jigsaw at 2000 feet over Dog channel." Jigsaw is the code name for the GCA controller, who, when contacted by the pilot would say:

"Baker Easy 34 this is Jigsaw. I receive you loud and clear. Turn left to a heading of 337 degrees, maintain 2000 feet. Landing will be into the west, altimeter 30.03, ceiling 500 overcast, visibility ½ mile, wind northwest at 7."

When the blip on the GCA operator's radarscope indicates that the plane is over the beacon that marks the beginning of the landing approach Jigsaw comes back:

"Baker Easy 34 now turn right to 90 degrees. Descend to 1500 feet."

On his radarscope the controller watches the plane holding this course and altitude until it is ready to turn into the base leg for approach to the landing, then advises the pilot:

"Baker Easy 34 now turn right to a heading of 180 degrees."

As the plane reaches the position to turn into its final approach and descent, Jigsaw advises the pilot to turn right to 260 degrees. This heading may vary slightly due to wind conditions and compensation for drift, but it will line the plane up approximately on a course to its final approach.

Up to this point, the plane has been controlled by an operator at a Planned Position Indicator. Now the plane is turned over to a final controller, using a Prescision Scope. After identifying himself and telling the pilot that he need not acknowledge further instructions the final controller says:

"Now turn to a heading of 270 degrees, you are slightly to the left of azimuth. [Azimuth is a line on the final controller's scope, directly in line with the runway.] Now that heading of 270 is bringing you back on azimuth. Now correct back left to 265 degrees. You are now six miles east of the runway, approaching the glide path; start rate of descent at 550 feet per minute. Your azimuth is good. The rate of descent is good. Now correct left to 261 degrees. You are now coming back on azimuth; correct back right to 264 degrees. You are drifting above the glide path, you are 50 feet high; increase your rate of descent. Your azimuth is good. You are three miles from touchdown. You are now approaching the glide path again; adjust your rate of descent to 550 feet per minute. Your azimuth is good. You are on the glide path; you are now two miles from touchdown. You have been cleared by the tower for a landing. You are now a mile and a half from touchdown. Your azimuth is good. You are drifting slightly below the glide path. You are 25 feet low. Adjust your rate of descent. Now turn left one degree. Heading should now be

263. You are back on the glide path. Resume normal rate of descent. You are one mile from touchdown. 263 is a good heading. Your azimuth is good. You are on the glide path. You are now three-quarter miles from touchdown. Steer further left 262. You are on the glide path. You are one-half mile from touchdown. You are on the glide path. Your azimuth is good. You are now approaching the end of the runway. You are on the glide path. You are 50 feet over the runway. Take over and land."

There had been close cooperation between the British and the Americans since the airlift started, but it was now apparent that the most efficient operation called for more than cooperation. The Americans had more planes than the British—particularly more big planes. The Gooney Birds were phased out by October, entirely replaced by C-54s, whereas the British were still using a majority of twin engine Dakotas because they did not have enough four engine planes. Replacing a Dakota with a C-54 tripled the tonnage per flight. Further, the northern and central corridors from the British zone to Gatow and back were shorter than the southern and central corridors from the American zone to Templehof and back; the flying time of the former was about an hour, on the latter about an hour and a half. Two planes based at Celle or Fassberg could do the work of three planes based at Rein-Main or Wiesbaden; two C-54s operating from the English bases were equal to nine twin engine planes operating from American bases.

Some C-54s had been operating out of Fassberg since early in August, but it was obvious that a combined administration with centralized control would materially increase efficiency. The idea was presented to Air Marshal Sir Arthur Sanders, General LeMay's opposite number, of completely combining Operation Vittles with Plane Fare into a single airlift under unified command. Sir Arthur was a little reluctant. Obviously the top command would have to be American, since almost 80 percent of the carrying capacity was American. However, the British commander saw the merit of the idea and agreed that his operation should be combined with the American lift, with General Tunner in overall command. This was probably the outstanding example of an integrated military operation between the two countries. Almost everything except flight crews were combined. Americans continued to fly American planes and Britons to fly English planes, but English ground crews served American planes, and English controllers brought them in. It worked flawlessly. In fact, there was less friction between British and American airlift personnel than between airlift headquarters and USAFE. The only difference that was recorded was the constant gripe of the Americans against the British mess. Americans did not consider porridge and kippers a fit breakfast, and the British did not take kindly to bacon and eggs.

As fall approached, the hectic, helter-skelter aspect of the early weeks of the airlift had changed to a pattern akin to an assembly line in an automobile plant, smoothly flowing, never ceasing. Under normal conditions the corridors now operated with four blocks of seventy planes each, the blocks from Rein-Main and Wiesbaden working the corridors alternately—when a block from the former was in the air the next block from the latter was being prepared at its home base. The stop watch and the statistical chart were the earmarks of a thoroughly business-like operation. Motion study engineers timed every aspect of handling the planes on the ground—loading and unloading, fueling, briefing, dispatching. New systems were tried and timed to find the best procedures for cutting turn-around time. New tie-down straps were developed, and metal cargo chutes were replaced with more sturdy hardwood ones. Loading and unloading time decreased as systems developed by motion study were introduced, until ten tons of cargo could be moved from a truck trailer to the cabin of a C-54, tied down in twenty minutes, and removed in thirteen. Over fifty charts in the Control Center at Headquarters constantly recorded every phase of the operation— turn-around times, engine availability, utilization of aircraft, flying hours per crew, and much more. And at every squadron there was a "Howgozit" chart to inform the men how their squadron was performing, in terms of tonnage, in relation to the total performance.

As efficiency increased, the daily tonnage into Berlin mounted. At the end of June, 1500 tons had seemed an impossible goal. With the advent of the first C-54s, it passed 3000. Two more squadrons of the big planes arrived with Tunner, six more in August, and by the end of that month the combined Anglo-American daily tonnage was above 5000—well over the minimum requirement of 4500 that was estimated as a survival level. To celebrate Air Force Day—September 18, 1948—a special twenty-four drive was put on that landed just short of 7000 tons of coal in the beleaguered city—a bonus that gave each family with small children in Berlin twenty-five pounds for household heating. A month later, the minimum requirements were raised to 5620 tons a day.

A factor in setting the record on September 18 was a single C-74 which was attached to the airlift. This was the first real transport plane that the Air Force owned, a four engine ship with a carrying capacity of twenty-five tons. On Air Force Day it was in the air twenty hours and made six round trips, instead of the usual four, landing 150 tons in Berlin by itself. Unfortunately, there were only eleven of these giants in existence and six of them were being modified. MATS was using some of the remaining five shuttling back and forth across the ocean to bring engines, parts, and other heavy equipment to the airlift. Tunner was fond of speculating that a full fleet of C-74s, flying from four bases in West Germany to two fields in Berlin, could have carried twenty-four thousand tons a day—far more than the normal requirements of the city—and, in addition, could have flown out everything that was manufactured there.

The C-74 was invaluable when the lift later flew in heavy equipment to build an airfield and a power plant; some of its units weighed 32,000 pounds. The single C-74 could not be integrated with the smaller planes on the airlift for routine use and was usually used for special jobs. Among the clumsy items that it carried were grand pianos coming out of Berlin. Occupation personnel had the right to take out their personal belongings when their tour of duty ended, and many of them had acquired grand pianos. Said Tunner: "It sometimes rankled us on Operations Vittles to fly out a grand piano and other loot for someone who probably had gone into Berlin with a duffel bag, but ours was not to reason why."

During the fall and on into the winter, the Russians continued to use rather childish forms of harassment. They staged antiaircraft practice with the plane towing the target flying along the edge of the corridor; sometimes the shells burst in the corridor. On other occasions, as airlift planes lumbered up the corridor, a Russian jet would zoom out of nowhere pulling a sleeve target, with another fighter pouring machine gun bullets into it. At times, individual Russian planes buzzed the transports. A particularly childish trick that they used once was to mount powerful searchlights at Gatow, where the Russian zone came almost to the end of the runway. They flashed these in the eyes of the pilots as they took off. All of this was annoying and unnerving, but the airlift pilots ignored them and flew steadily on.

The Russians did not do any of the many things that they might have done—short of attacking the airlift planes—to seriously hamper the operation of the airlift. It would have been technically possible for them to jam radio communications in the corridor or interfere with the operation of radarscope, making instrument flying impossible. There were some points at which they could have raised barrage balloons which might have swung over the corridors. It was obvious that they would not risk the development of the Berlin crisis into an armed conflict.

Tunner had his own opinion why the Russians never seriously tried to interfere with the airlift. They were, he said, so completely confident that it could not succeed. This was partly based on their observation of the German experience at Stalingrad. Field Marshal Hermann Goering had assured Hitler that the *Luftwaffe* could air supply the army that was surrounded there with 300 tons a day. They never succeeded in delivering more than ninety tons, and they lost 300 planes. Their failure was not through lack of planes, of which they had more than 500. Their principal faults were the absence of know-how and inadequate maintenance: a particular problem in the Russian winter with planes that they had brought from the desert campaign in North Africa.

Another factor that bolstered the Russian conviction that the airlift could not succeed was that their airmen did not then understand instrument flying. When there was a low overcast airlift planes never saw Soviet fighters above the clouds. The Russians were good flyers, capable of all kinds of stunts, and they flew in bad weather—but always below the clouds. Because they had not yet mastered the technique of instrument flying, they were sure that the long German winter, with its almost continuous overcast, would stop the airlift. They were not alone in this. Both the Berlin and the American press were equally pessimistic. But when he was queried in the late fall, Tunner quietly replied: "We're well along with our winterization program. We'll fly Vittles as long as the United States government wants it flown."

SIX

The Impossible Does Not Take Longer

Icing has always been a dangerous problem in flying. Usually this happens in the air when moisture from clouds condenses on the forward edges of the wings of a plane, coating them with a layer of ice which affects the contour of the plane aerodynamically by changing the shape of the wing. Advanced technology has developed ways of coping with this by means of a deicer that pulsates to crack the ice when it forms.

But deicers do not work when the plane is standing on the ground with its engines idle, and in rainswept Berlin ice frequently formed on planes while they were being conditioned, loaded, and fueled, making a heavily loaded take-off hazardous. The great know-how of the aviation industry back home could easily have devised a means to cope with this condition—given time. But the coal, potatoes, and powdered milk that Berliners needed to stay alive would not wait.

So a sergeant in a ground crew figured out an answer that could be put into effect overnight. There were a couple of decommissioned jet fighter plane engines available. "Why not," reasoned the unknown improvisor, "mount the jets on small trucks and heat the wings with their exhausts as the trucks moved slowly along?" It worked perfectly and on days when icing conditions prevailed, the airlift planes took off with warm wings.

There were countless instances of this type of ingenuity on the airlift which involved improvisation based on skill and know-how. Much of it came from the lower echelons of personnel and included many little things that were not vital in themselves but that added up to a major improvement in the efficiency of this complex operation. The unusual short-haul runs were tough on spark plugs, which were being changed at a rate that would keep a factory busy to supply them, until a mechanic devised a simple spark plug reconditioning tool that saved over 40,000 plugs a month. Coal dust was a nuisance and a hazard, and in the early days of the lift, the cabin floors of coal-carrying planes were sometimes ankle deep in it. A partial solution to this was very simple—after somebody thought of it. The floors of the cabins were covered with tarpaulins, which were removed and shaken out at Templehof. And the dust, a usable fuel, was saved—over 500 tons of it, the equivalent of fifty plane loads of coal.

In at least one instance the planes were reengineered at Rein-Main, and an improvement was built in to better adapt them to airlift duty. It was found that leaking gas tanks were far move prevalent than in normal use. Engineers figured that this might be caused by the small loads of gas that the planes carried. To fill the tanks to capacity for the short round trip to Berlin would have meant carrying hundred of pounds of unnecessary weight—a full load of gas would carry the plane some 3000 miles, so the tanks were loaded to only 20 percent of capacity. The small amount of gas in the bottoms of the tanks was constantly sloshing back and forth, and it was reasoned that this was causing leaks at seams. A drafting board was set up and an ingenious system of baffles designed to keep the gas from moving rapidly back and forth in the tank. These were installed at Obie, and one more problem was licked.

Perhaps the man who contributed most to help the airlift do the impossible quickly was a civilian named H. P. Lacomb. Before World War II, Lacomb had been a welder. During the war, he worked for the Air Force as a civilian at his regular work until he became involved in building an air base at Natal in Brazil. Large earth-moving equipment was needed at the construction site. There was no way to get it there except by plane, and most of it was too big to fit into a plane. Lacomb's genius with an oxyacetylene torch provided the answer. In Florida he cut the monster machines apart into jigsaw pieces that would fit into a plane. Then he boarded the plane with the pieces and flew to Brazil, where he patiently welded them back together again.

Early in the airlift it was realized that a third runway was a vital necessity at Templehof. There was plenty of room for it, but a runway that would withstand the beating of the blows delivered by the airlift planes landing at three-minute intervals with a gross weight of 70,000 pounds could not be built with picks and shovels. For such construction heavy equipment was required—graders, bulldozers, rollers, scrapers, stone crushers, and more. There was no such equipment in Berlin; the Russians had taken it. And such machinery would not fit even in the giant C-74. It seemed that the success of the airlift might be curtailed for want of a strip of asphalt—until somebody remembered Lacomb. What he could do in the jungle of Brazil he could surely do in Berlin.

There was not much demand for Lacomb's unusual skill in peace time, and he had left his job with the Air Force at the end of the war. With the help of the F.B.I., he was located working at an obscure job at an airport in the Mid-west—he apparently had developed a taste for being around planes. Overnight, MATS whipped Lacomb and his torches to Rein-Main.

Lacomb handled the first few pieces of earth-moving equipment himself. While a curious crowd watched, he walked around a monstrous bulldozer, marking it into sections with chalk. For reasons that only Lacomb knew, it was important where the cuts were made. Then he donned his face-protecting mask, lit the blue flame of his torch, and applied it at the end of a chalk line. The shower of sparks fascinated the onlookers for a while, but it was slow work, and they soon drifted away. When they returned the next day the ground was covered with pieces of two mammoth earth-moving machines, each piece small enough to fit into the C-74 and light enough to handle. Lacomb then boarded the plane with the pieces, flew to Templehof, and applied a welding rod ahead of the flame of his torch to put the pieces back together again.

The genius of the torch then set up a school to train others in his skill. Soon there was a cutting-apart crew at Rein-Main and a putting-together crew at Templehof. After they were trained, there was nothing that was too big to fly to Berlin. This system later made it possible to reequip the power house in the west sector that the Russians had stripped by sending mammoth generators in pieces. When this generating plant, the largest in Berlin, got back into production one of the worst hardships of the blockade was at least partially overcome.

Since its inception, the airlift had faced all kinds of bottlenecks. A shortage of crews for the first planes that were available; then a shortage of planes; then a renewed shortage of crews; a shortage of parts, of engines, of gas; and always a shortage of earthbound facilities and personnel. By the end of the summer a new shortage loomed —a shortage of airports in Berlin. The new runway at Templehof made it possible to make full use of all the planes that were then in use and maintain a headway of a landing or a takeoff every ninety seconds. But additional planes would soon be available and when they arrived the two Berlin airports would not provide enough runways to accommodate them. Templehof could not be expanded beyond its three runways; Gatow had no room for more than the two runways that it already had. To make full use of the planes, it was necessary to create a third airport.

There was an ideal location for a landing field in the French zone—a rolling field near Tegel forest approximately 4000 by 8000 feet almost totally unobstructed around the edges. This had been used as a training site for Hermann Goering's antiaircraft divisions, and rusted guns still dotted it, their slim barrels pointing skyward like futuristic scarecrows. The French were quite willing to let the Americans build a field there—if they could.

Under normal conditions this would be a routine engineering and construction job, involving the leveling of the field by pulling out stumps and rocks, gouging out a long, level trough, laying a two-foot base of concrete, and topping it with a smooth concrete or asphalt surface. But conditions in Berlin were far from normal. The concrete that would ordinarily be used did not exist in Berlin and to fly it in would deprive Berliners of thousands of tons of food and fuel for weeks. The only equipment available were a few pre-World War I steam rollers that were so decrepit that the Russians had not thought it worth while to take them. The equipment problem could be solved by Lacomb and his crews. They cut apart and reassembled eighty-one mammoth tractors, bulldozers, rollers, and graders.

Getting material for the runway was a more acute problem until some army engineer realized that Berlin had a possible substitute for concrete in great abundance. Much of the city was covered with piles of bricks from bombed buildings. "Why not," reasoned a construction engineer, "lay six-inch layers of bricks in the foundation excavation, pulverize them by running tractors over them, and then compact them with rollers." This would provide a base as solid as concrete.

A runway 5500 feet by 150 feet, with 500-foot overruns at each end, would require upwards of ten million bricks, the equivalent of ten city blocks, and while mechanical equipment would crush them, it would not move them from rubble piles around the city into layers in a trench at Tegel. That had to be done by hand. Each individual brick must be picked up or pried out of a broken wall, thrown into a truck, transported to the site, and then laid in a six-inch layer; a process that had to be repeated four times to get the two-foot base that the runway required. It was a manual material moving job that matched the building of the Burma Road with coolies.

A call went out to the people of Berlin for volunteers. The pay offered was one mark twenty pfennigs, hardly a living wage. A further inducement, and perhaps a more important one, was a good hot meal for each shift. But the principal reason that 17,000 Berliners turned out to work around-the-clock in three shifts was unquestionably emotional rather than material. This was their airlift. They wanted to be a part of it, to contribute their labor to making it work. This was evident from the zeal with which they tackled the job and kept at it in all kinds of weather and from the character of the people who composed the labor force. The workers were approximately 60 percent men and 40 percent women, from every walk of life. Stolid peasants wearing wooden shoes worked side by side with soft-handed women wearing silk dresses. Common laborers were mixed with ex-army officers, scientists, and teachers. Bricks were picked up by manicured hands and passed to hands that were used to typing, or cooking, or drafting, or playing an instrument.

Every imaginable costume could be found on the workers at Tegel. They had no work clothes, as such—they wore the only clothes they had. During the hot days of September, when the project got under way, bathing trunks and beach costumes were much in evidence, and the favorite targets for photographers were a few shapely *Fräuleins* wearing bikinis to handle bricks. Officially, the field was built by army engineers but there were only fifteen engineer officers and 150 enlisted men to run the heavy equipment. The rest of the job was done, by hand, by 17,000 Berliners.

Specifications called for the foundation to be topped with a layer of crushed stone bonded with asphalt. Ten thousand barrels of asphalt and a cut-apart stone crusher were flown in, and the Berliners turned to prying up cobble stones from blocked-off streets to feed the stone crusher. A small amount of crushed stone was already available in the form of ballast for unused railway spurs in the west sector. Over the screaming protest of the Soviets, who operated the railways, these spurs were ripped up, and the ballast was added to the runway. By this time Russian protests had lost their threat.

When the construction of Tegel started on September 5, a target date of January 1 was set for its completion. After watching the Berliners work, this target was lowered to December 15. The first plane landed at Tegel on November 5. The job, which would have normally taken four months, was completed in half that time due to the diligence of the German labor force; and an independent testing laboratory found that the runway was stronger than the average runway built in the States.

Tegel became the chief terminal for British tankers flying diesel oil, kerosene, and gasoline, and part of the installation were four large underground fuel storage tanks connected by pipeline to ten stations at which tankers could be drained simultaneously. The entire field was designed to meet airlift conditions, with unloading stations that had truck bed-high platforms upon which cargo could be unloaded by gravity and rolled on to trucks.

There was only one obstruction on the approaches to

Tegel—the transmission tower of the Berlin radio station.
Although the tower was in the French sector and the station itself in the British, the operation had been controlled
by the Russians since their entry into the city and was run
by German personnel under Soviet supervision. Before the
field was completed, the French commandant in Berlin,
General Ganeval, had written to the city council in the
east sector, which presumably had authority over the station, although the actual control lay with the Russians.
His letter asking that the tower be moved because it was
a hazard to the use of the Tegel field was ignored. When
the field opened the request was made again, and this time
it was refused.

A few days later General Ganeval invited the American
detachment stationed at Tegel, some twenty individuals,
to come to his office for a mysterious meeting. When they
arrived, he locked the door and started to serve refresh-
ments. The Americans were confused but Ganeval's Gallic
charm prevented them from insisting on an explanation.
They did not know that while they drank his champagne,
French engineers were placing demolition charges at the
base of the tower. Suddenly, a mighty blast rattled the windows and shook the room, and the Americans dashed to
the windows in time to see the 200-foot tower slowly topple
to the ground. "You will have no more trouble with the
tower," said the smiling Ganeval.

From the East German government and Soviet headquarters came strong protests; the Russians, of course,
blamed the whole thing on the Americans. But the Americans, thanks to Ganeval's foresight, had a perfect alibi.
They were under lock and key when it happened. Under

the headline, "Berlin Indignant Over Act of Violence," the Communist-controlled press branded the destruction of the tower as an act of "cultural barbarism" carried out at American command and as a disgrace to France. Paris reprimanded General Ganeval, but the thing was a *fait accompli,* and there was nothing that could be done about it. Ganeval later reported that Kotikov called on him, shortly after the tower was demolished, in a towering rage. After screaming "saboteur" he quieted down and said:

"Why didn't you get in touch with me? We would surely have been able to reach some agreement."

"I don't think so," replied the French General. "Not after you broke your promise to me." The reference here was to the west sector police for whom Kotikov had given Ganeval a safe conduct when they were surrounded in the City Hall and who had been arrested forthwith when they left. Blowing up the tower was the General's revenge.

As he left, Kotikov turned at the door and said, "This airfield may well cost you French dear."

"Undoubtedly," replied the General, "airfields are expensive. But peace is after all very precious."

By mid-fall ground-based flying aids had been improved by the latest equipment flown from the States by MATS. The most modern radio beacons and communications equipment were installed to replace the obsolete types on which the pilots had to depend in the early summer. One top priority item was a system of high-intensity approach lighting at Templehof. Despite the improvement in GCA landing techniques, the situation at the Berlin field was such that all possible types of advanced landing aids were desirable. High intensity lighting equipment scheduled for installation at commercial fields in the States was diverted to Germany.

The problem at Templehof was where to put it. Approach lighting is designed for installation at ground level, with the path of lights extending out from the end of the runway. Because of the buildings surrounding Templehof, this would not work; lights at ground level could not be seen by pilots approaching the field until they passed over the apartment houses and were almost over the field. A system was devised for placing the lights on towers of gradually increasing height, starting low at the end of the runway and ascending to an outer tower seventy-five feet high. When it came to building the towers the problem of materials again arose. Flying in construction materials would take valuable cargo space from food and fuel, and building them of brick would be a long operation requiring scarce skilled labor. The answer was found underfoot by another improvisation. When the runways at Templehof had been rebuilt, the metal landing mats with which the one surfaced runway had originally been covered were replaced by asphalt. Now these large, perforated steel plates were cut into strips and welded back together again in the form of towers.

The only possible location for the path of approach lighting was through the cemetery adjacent to one of the main runways. This meant that the cemetery would contain two rows of unsightly towers and several graves would have to be moved to make room for their emplacement. The Berlin city government gave permission to move the graves, but this made fine propaganda material for the Communist press. A picture was published showing the cemetery surrounded by barbed wire with a caption saying that Berliners could witness the desecration of the graves of their sacred dead by the American warmongers only from a distance. The newspaper story said: "In a reckless manner, holes and long cable ducts have been dug and masts erected. The Americans behave in Berlin like troops engaged in a war in an enemy country." The Soviet indignation rose to fever pitch when it was found necessary to remove the steeple of a small church that obscured a view of the light path. Even a house of God was not safe from the depredations of the American barbarians. The Russians were the only ones to complain about this. The congregation of the church in question was quite happy with the new roof design created for the building by a prominent German architect and installed at American expense.

The historic pattern of handling heavy freight has been from ship, to rail head, to trucking point. There was no provision in any system for the participation of an airplane. In the early days of the lift when relatively small tonnage was involved the only system was to keep the freight moving forward in the hope that a load would be there when a plane was ready for it. But this hit or miss method would not handle upwards of five or six hundred flights a day. The steady beat of the block system, with takeoffs at three-minute intervals, could not be maintained if a plane had to wait for a load. Also, it often happened that some loads did not make full use of the plane's carrying capacity. Six tons of macaroni filled the plane's cargo space but was 8000 pounds under the maximum weight limit; whereas ten tons of sugar filled but a portion of the cabin. For full utilization and maximum maintenance of schedule, it was necessary to develop a system under which a plane and its load would reach the loading point at the same time and the products in the load would be "married" so that each plane carried its total capacity on every trip.

By the fall of the year the airlift was drawing supplies from all corners of the globe: butter from Denmark, coffee from Brazil, sugar from Cuba, wheat from Minnesota, coal from the Ruhr. Getting these diverse products to a specific point on an airfield at a given minute in ten-ton units of assorted material that made best use of the plane's capacity was a job of tremendous complexity that was handled by the Army Transportation Corps.

To supply the fields in the American zone freight, whether it originated from ship, barge or rail, was routed through the Frankfort marshaling yards and forwarded to Rein-Main or Wiesbaden by rail. At both bases, warehouses had been built at each railhead to store a three-day supply, so that a constant flow of all products would be available. Trailers, with the same ten-ton capacity as the planes, backed up to freight car or warehouse platforms and were loaded in accordance with how the load was to be placed aboard the plane. Most food cargoes were "married" at the time the trailer was loaded. A particular trailer might take four tons of sugar from a freight car and then move to a warehouse for six tons of macaroni. The sugar was placed in the center of the trailer and the macaroni around the sides. After a pause at a weighing scale, the loaded trailer then took its place in the ready line.

A pilot returning from Berlin with an empty plane reported his estimated time of arrival and his hardstand number to the control tower by radio. This information was transmitted to the communications shack on the ready-line, and a loaded trailer was dispatched to meet the plane when it landed, carrying its crew of D.P.s and two supervisors, one from the Transportation Corps and the other from the airlift task force. The transportation man stayed in the bed of the trailer to supervise unloading; the task force man went aboard the plane to supervise the placing of the load in accordance with a weight distribution chart. Both supervised the tiedown, which was rechecked by the plane's crew.

All of this may sound simple, but when it is realized that it meant loading and handling upwards of five hundred trucks a day—ultimately eight or nine hundred—with an assortment of over one hundred products in food stuffs and medicines alone—not to mention special loads of newsprint, asphalt, coal, tools, and much more—it was obviously a job that required a genius for organization. Yet in almost every case the plane, the trailer with its load, and a fuel truck arrived at the hardstand within the same minute.

One thing that could not be organized was the weather, which represented the greatest single threat to the successful operation of the airlift. German winter weather was notoriously bad. It was also notoriously freakish, subject to rapid change and to a variation of conditions at opposite ends of the route. Nothing could be done to change the weather, but much could be done to anticipate it and plan accordingly. The weather service that was set up for the lift operation was more elaborate and extensive than any forecasting service ever developed.

There were two aspects to the forecasting—a weather service for planning purposes and another for actual flying operations. The former started in the arctic, whence a permanent weather ship sent hourly reports directly to a central weather station at Rein-Main. There were half a dozen more of these ships in the North Atlantic and one off the coast of Spain. Reports came in from scores of land-based weather observation points in Europe and on the coast of Canada. In addition, the British maintained a flying weather patrol over the ocean north, west, and south of the British Isles, sending reports to the airlift at thirty-minute intervals. Four American B-29 bombers were added to this British patrol, especially for the airlift forecasting. All of this data funneling into Rein-Main was the basis for a four-day forecast and a twenty-four-hour forecast.

For operational weather information there were five observatories at the main British and American fields and in Berlin, connected by teletype. During conditions of overcast, each of these worked constantly with electronic instruments and balloons to determine conditions at various altitudes. In addition, starting in the fall when bad weather was the rule, every seventh plane carried a radio man who reported weather conditions at four specific points along the route. The weather men at all five observatories held telephone conferences three times a day and gave a forecast to operations for the hours immediately ahead. Between conference times they were in almost continuous contact with traffic controllers to supply them with minute by minute changes in the weather along the corridors.

None of this made it possible to fly when visibility was zero—there were periods when the lift was closed down.

But the long-range forecast made it possible to schedule planes for maintenance work when such periods were coming, and the operational forecast and constant flow of information permitted planes to take off in sub-operational conditions if they were flying toward improving weather or to hold up when the weather at their destination would not permit the completion of the flight.

Historically, November was the worst month of the year for weather, and November 1948, was no exception. Weather conditions on fifteen out of the thirty days made flying almost impossible. December was a little better, but not much. For the first time, the airlift faltered during these two months despite the fact that, with the arrival of the last squadrons of C-54s in October and the opening of the Tegel field, airlift capacity was at its peak. But tonnage hit a new high in January and for every month thereafter. The fear that had been in the back of Berliners' minds during the summer that the airlift could not function during winter weather was dispelled when, on November 1st, in defiance of the worst weather of the year, the food ration was increased by 20 percent to a level that was approximately 220 calories per day higher than the ration before the blockade.

SEVEN

Candy and Schmoos and Camels and Things

To Berliners—or at least to young Berliners—the best known man on the airlift was not General Tunner nor General Le May. He was a prematurely bald, twenty-seven-year-old bachelor from Garland, Utah, Lieutenant Gail S. Halverson, who was known to every kid in Berlin as the "Chockolade Flier." Halverson had been a ferry pilot during the war. When the airlift started, his MATS outfit, the 17th Air Transport Squadron, was stationed at Mobile, Alabama. They departed for Berlin in such a hurry that Halverson had left his car parked under a tree and had hidden the keys.

The lieutenant was crazy about kids. He hoped some day to have eight or ten of his own, if he ever got back to Utah to pop the question to the girl who was waiting. Meanwhile he befriended every youngster who came his way. During his ferrying days he had walked through towns in Africa, Italy, and South America with queues of kids trailing along behind him begging for the candy and gum with which his pockets were stuffed. In the fall of 1948, on a day off, he took a walk in Berlin. This was somewhat un-

146

usual for airlift pilots, most of whom merely turned around at Templehof and spent their free time in Frankfort. The ever-present kids who gathered around gave him an idea which developed into "Little Vittles," an aspect of the airlift that received world-wide publicity. Halverson described the inception of it as follows.

"Down in Africa and Italy all through the war, and in South America cities since the war ended, I always got snowed under by kids swarming around wanting gum and candy and, naturally, cigarettes. I don't smoke or drink, so I can't indulge their wilder vices, but usually I have candy and gum in my pockets.

"Well, I'm telling now about Berlin. I got in the middle of all these kids and what do you think happened? None of them jerked at my pants or threatened to knock my block off. They wanted to hold a polite conversation and try out their English on me. Their English is about as bad as my German. After about an hour, in which I gained considerable stature as an airlift pilot, I noticed something was missing. I couldn't put my finger on it, but it nagged me. And finally I realized what it was. Those kids hadn't begged for a single thing.

"It took another hour of crossbreeding our languages to find out it wasn't lack of candy-hunger that held them back; they just lacked the brass other kids have. So I told them to be down at the end of the runway next day, and I'd drop them some gum and candy. That night I tied up some candy bars and gum in handkerchiefs and had my chief sling them out on a signal from me next day. Day by day the crowds of kids waiting for the drop got bigger, and day by day my supply of old shirts, G.I. sheets, and old shorts, all of which I used for parachutes, got smaller."

Halverson told this story before his project became world-famous and ended it by saying: "My car is in Mobile, all my handkerchiefs are in Berlin, and my heart is in Utah. How I'm ever going to get out there and remain long enough to talk her into marriage, I don't know. And I've got practically no hair left to tear out worrying about, big as the problem is."

"Little Vittles" gradually grew beyond a one-man show. First other pilots in his squadron joined him in the candy drop, then it spread to other squadrons. PX stocks of candy and gum became depleted as pilots and ground crewmen donated their money and their laundry to the cause. During their free time, husky mechanics and virile pilots sat on the sides of their bunks making little parachutes for the next day's drop.

In the States, newspaper stories about the private airlift for children caught the public fancy, and after Halverson was flown back briefly to appear on a national radio show, his squadron at Rein-Main was flooded with tons of candy and thousands of handkerchiefs, some of them already made into parachutes. Girl Scout troops and women's clubs made collecting for Little Vittles a project, and some candy manufacturers contributed their products in bulk. The candy airlift peaked one day in the spring when the airlift detachment at Templehof arranged a picnic for thousands of Berlin kids on Peacock Island in Lake Hegel with a mass candy drop as the major event.

The daily drop was made over the cemetery adjacent to Templehof, where the children waited for the planes. The

Russian press, of course, pointed out that the lack of re-spect for the dead shown in the kids running around the graves, was another indication of American barbarism. At Christmas, Halverson received over 4000 cards and letters from the grateful children of Berlin.

Children, particularly, considered the airlift as *their* air-lift, a part of their lives, not some external phenomenon. The airlift played a central part in their lives, and the planes became a natural focus for their imaginative play. Recalled one Berliner: "When they travel in the elevated past Templehof airfield, all Berlin children wish that the train would go slower. They would like to see a little more of the airlift, which for weeks has been the center of their conversations, their games, and perhaps their dreams."

When school children were asked to draw pictures of the airlift almost all of them showed Berliners participating in the airlift in some way. One youngster drew a picture of a family, complete with cat and dog, standing on the roof of their house looking up at parachutes floating down from an airlift plane above, each with an appropriate gift for a member of the family: a bone for the dog, a mouse for the cat, a toy train for the little boy, and a food package for Momma and Papa.

Children made up a large part of the crowds that thronged to the airport to watch the planes come in and created a special problem for the M.P.s as they tried to sneak in to get closer to the planes and talk to the pilots. At certain times they were permitted on the field, and Air Force personnel showed them through the planes. Usually, if there was a photographer around, a pretty little girl with a bouquet of flowers or a cute boy clutching a puppy or a kitten that he wanted to give to a pilot, could get in—the Air Force is very publicity minded. One youngster climbed the fence at Templehof and thrust a package into the hands of a pilot with a note that read: "Dear Pilots; I am a boy twelve years old, and I would like for you to have this airplane that I carved with my jackknife. I am presenting this for all the good deeds you have done for our beloved home town of Berlin night and day." Some members of the airlift task force made model planes as a hobby—there was little else to do in recreation-starved Rein-Main—and gave them to Berlin kids at Templehof.

The lake where the British flying boats landed was also a magnet for the young. One boy later remembered that: "One day there was another novelty for us children, which all the newspapers featured with pictures and headlines. The British introduced a type of aircraft into the airlift which was entirely new to us. It was the Sunderland 'flying boat,' which landed in the water near Schwanenwerder. But only a few landed each day. We often begged our parents to arrange our Sunday afternoon walk in such a way that, after going through the woods, we arrived at the water. There it was usually some time before a plane, heralded by the cries and gestures of the children, landed on the water. With interest we followed the unloading and loading. We longed to be allowed to fly in one of these water birds."

What the airlift meant to the children of Berlin was expressed in the recollection of a sixteen-year-old, written some five years later: "In spite of all these vitally important flights, the Americans remembered, as they had many times before, to make the children happy. On a beautiful, clear, sunny weekday a large crowd of children swarmed around the entrance to the airfield. They had been allowed to leave school earlier than usual because the airfield had been thrown open to visitors. In droves, the children threw themselves upon the planes, each according to his own interest, or got friendly 'Amis' to explain other things to him. In the afternoon came the surprise. A transport machine landed, and a living camel got out. The same machine brought a large quantity of candy, which was thrown to the jubilant bunch of children. Until late in the evening the small fry, with chocolate smeared over their faces, talked about the wonderful day."

The camel, whose name was Clarence, was the brainchild of Lieutenant Donald Butterfield who bought it, and a donkey, in North Africa and flew the animals back to Germany. Using Clarence as a symbol, the Air Force organized a project, obviously called "Camel Caravan," to collect food and other gifts from families in West Germany for the children of the blockaded capital. Before the project got off the ground—literally or figuratively—tragedy struck when the donkey kicked Clarence, breaking a leg. The camel had to be shot. Lieutenant Butterfield then acquired another camel, which was also named Clarence, although it later developed that it should have been named Clarissa.

In a C-47, prominently labeled Camel Caravan, the new Clarence flew to Berlin with three tons of gifts. After posing for pictures and patiently giving rides to kids at Templehof, the camel returned to make a personal-appearance tour of West Germany canvassing for more presents for the children of the blockaded city.

Gifts for the people of Berlin from West Germany and from all parts of the free world became such a sizable portion of airborne cargo that the airlift finally had to refuse to carry individual gift parcels. They were taking too much space from the more efficiently packed bulk cargoes. A system was set up under which gift parcels were sent to a central pool in West Germany where their contents were repacked to make more practical plane loads.

Throughout West Germany a special two pfennig stamp was required in addition to the regular postage stamp, proceeds from the sale of which were used to buy supplies for Berlin. Later, special "Help Berlin" ten and twenty pfennig stamps were placed on sale for voluntary use. Citizens of Westphalia and Saxony went on a one-day fast and contributed the day's food ration, plus 100,000 tons of coal to Berlin. The city of Bremen donated twenty million cigarettes. Hamburg sent a collection of urgently needed medical supplies to which the Bavarian Red Cross added a ton of medicines. In Munich the Simpl Cabaret had a Berlin Night Benefit to support Berlin entertainers. Citizens of Westphalia also collected 10,000 candles which were flown to the blacked-out capital. Schleswig-Holstein sent two million pine tree seedlings to replace the trees that had been bombed or cut down in Berlin.

Private individuals in the United States contributed an average of 600 CARE packages a day, a total of over 200,000. American trade unions sent 1000 twenty-pound food parcels to their fellow unionists in Berlin. The students of Stanford University in California sent fifteen tons of food to the students of the five West Berlin Universities and Colleges. Americans in the Military Government at

Hesse collected 2000 pounds of food for children at a summer camp. The American Army donated 4000 technical volumes to help establish a library at the Free University. The Army Medical Corps rushed quantities of vaccine, refrigerated in Coca-Cola bottles, to prevent an epidemic of a kind of sleeping sickness among the city's horses. Airlift pilots contributed fresh bananas and flew them to hospitalized children suffering from a rare disease. One pilot, Captain Kenneth Salls, went hunting on his day off in the Spessart Mountains near Frankfort and flew the 290 pounds of meat from the ten point stag that he bagged to the patients of a hospital in Berlin.

The National Institute of Diaper Services of America offered a very special gift to the mothers of infants in Berlin; they would donate 12,000 diapers a week to be flown in by the airlift, which would also fly out the soiled ones for laundering. Airlift officials, none of whom had to wash diapers, refused this generous offer.

Relief agencies throughout the world helped to furnish Berlin with various supplies to augment those provided by the government. The International Red Cross, the Society of Friends, the Menonites, CARE, the Swedish Red Cross, UNICEF, the Swiss Red Cross, the Mormons, and the Adventists were among the most active. And these humanitarian groups were unconcerned with politics in the distribution of their largess. Over a third of their supplies went to people in the Russian zone. Even in the case of these charities, the Russians denied to West Berliners the goods that they provided.

The Swedish Red Cross had been bringing in food for 20,000 needy children since the occupation of the city.

Now the Russians stopped this distribution in the western sectors. A project of the International Red Cross involving an old-age feeding program was likewise forbidden outside the Soviet zone. The humanitarian agencies abandoned both projects in disgust. Early in January the Soviets turned back fifteen freight car loads of gift packages from America which had come to Germany by way of Sweden.

The most imaginative private gift was conceived by the personnel of one airlift squadron. This started with a telegram to cartoonist Al Capp, creator of Li'l Abner, who had recently added the Schmoo to the characters in Dog Patch. The Schmoo was a lovable little pear-shaped roly-poly fellow who was dedicated to the welfare of mankind in that he could be turned into any necessity or luxury. He gladly offered himself to be eaten, and if the diner wanted chicken, he tasted like chicken; if one wanted beef, he tasted like beef, or ice cream, or apple pie. You could build a house out of a Schmoo or make him into dresses or shoes. You could even turn him into currency or gold. There was nothing that the fantastic Schmoo could not do to cure man's ills.

In reply to the telegram, Capp willingly agreed to have the Schmoo help Berliners. The men of the squadron chipped in to buy 100 CARE packages and got an equal number of inflated Schmoos, which were sold as toys in the States. One bright afternoon these odd shaped balloon-like dolls floated to the ground near Templehof, each bearing a card on which was printed: "Hello. I'm a Schmoo. Perhaps you've never heard of me. In America I'm fairly famous as a fabulous creature who does only good for

people. Take me to a CARE office, and you'll see how fast
I can change into a CARE package."

Gift giving was a two-way proposition as Berliners continued to try to show their appreciation to the airlift in
many touching ways. Women, children, and oldsters
brought a variety of presents for the pilots to the gates of
the airfields, ranging from Schnauzer puppies, hand-knit
mufflers, paintings, china, and family heirlooms, to pastry
baked with the precious flour that the recipients were flying in. One Berlin masseur put an advertisement in *The
Task Force Times* offering to supply "free massage to all
fliers who arrive in Berlin with tired and stiff backs." One
pilot wrote, "Seems to me I've met every German in Berlin.
They come down here, clutching extremely valuable heirlooms against their breasts, and want to make a little ceremony of giving the stuff to the pilots. Or some child will
show up with flowers or a valued picture book. It's no act,
either."

A small item of cargo that meant a lot to Berliners was
animal food. One act of the Russians that had contributed
to changing the people's fear to anger in the early days of
the blockade had been the refusal to supply food for seeing-
eye dogs. The airlift had carried such food from the first,
and as soon as the need was recognized, added food for the
animals in the zoo, for animals used for scientific research,
for performing animals, and for police dogs.

There was, sadly, no food for pets. Berliners were great
dog lovers, and thousands had made sacrifices to keep their
pets alive through the war and the first years of the occupation. They would not be defeated now. Dog and cat
owners lined up outside American army kitchens to share

the scraps from the garbage. Dignified Berliners walked miles to the suburban residential sections in which the occupation forces lived to root in private garbage pails or to frankly beg at doors for food for their animals. Pride would not permit them to beg for themselves, but pride could be swallowed for the sake of their pets. It is possible that some dachshunds never ate as well before the blockade.

Some stray animals did not fare so well. Undoubtedly a great many of them were eaten during the blockade. One reporter told of standing on a corner of the Kurfürstendamm beside an old man with a little cart who kept calling out: "Hot frankfurters, hot frankfurters, only six pfennigs each."

A woman stopped and asked: "Are they real pork?"

"Of course," the man answered. And then in a whisper, so that a passer-by might not hear, he added: "There's a little fish mixed in, but anybody who did not know it wouldn't notice."

"Do you mean bow-wow?" the woman asked.

Then the passer-by spoke up: "Meow-meow is more like it."

Every time one of these stories about dogs and cats being converted into sausage appeared in the press, the paper received a shower of letters from outraged readers. One commentator noted that these people had written no such letters a few years before, when Jews, rather than dogs and cats, were killed. However, this was an indication of the difference between National Socialism and Western democracy, rather than evidence of callousness on the part of Berliners. Under the Nazis such a letter of protest would have been the writer's passport to a concentration camp.

Another item of cargo during the winter was a constant procession of V.I.P.s. The breakdown of the 5260-ton daily minimum quota established in October contained an item of thirty tons for "people." This represented an average of about 350 people a day who flew into Berlin. The airlift had great appeal to the leaders, prominent politicians, military men, and well-known journalists from many lands. Most of them did not get any special red carpet treatment. One load of V.I.P.s landed at Wiesbaden for lunch en route to Berlin and came back to find their plane full of flour.

American visitors included Vice President Alben Barkley, Ambassador to England Lewis Douglas, roving Ambassador Averell Harriman, Secretary of the Army Kenneth Royal, and Secretary of the Air Force Stuart Symington. From England came Prime Minister Clement Attlee, Foreign Minister Ernest Bevin, Anthony Eden, Secretary of State Arthur Henderson, and the RAF chief, Air Marshal Tedder.

The British Prime Minister arrived on an unfortunate day. While he was en route from England, winds of gale force developed in Berlin, blowing across the runways. The British at that time did not have a single plane on the airlift with a nose wheel landing gear. All of their planes had tail wheels or tail skids, making a cross-wind landing much more dangerous. All American planes had nose wheels, and these could continue to operate after the British planes were grounded, so the Prime Minister was landed at Rein-Main and transferred to an American plane. The British brass was lined up at Gatow to receive him with a band and honor guard, when the lone American plane landed, and Attlee descended in a cloud of coal dust—he had come in with a load of coal. "Why," the Prime Minister demanded sternly, "don't our planes have nose wheels?" Senior officers of the RAF assured him that they would look into it immediately.

General Tunner told an amusing story about the visit of Foreign Minister Ernest Bevin, a very big, gruff and precise man. On a tour of inspection Tunner took him to the control center and proudly started to explain the fifty charts that lined the walls, one of which was labeled "Organizational Chart." Bevin interrupted at the start of the lecture to growl: "What kind of a word is that? Organizational! There is no such word in the English language as organizational. You Americans made it up."

Later Tunner showed the Foreign Minister a C-97 that was visiting for a few days. This was the prototype of a giant double-decked craft that was known in commercial aviation as the Stratocruiser. After talking to the crew beside the plane, Tunner asked Bevin if he would like to go aboard and see the cockpit. The Prime Minister had recently recovered from a heart attack, and the cockpit was on the upper deck, reached by a vertical ladder. His staff protested at the exertion required to reach it, but Bevin ignored them and started toward the ladder. As he did, a young American airman jumped in front of him to go up first to open the three-foot hatch at the top and help the Foreign Minister up. This thoughtful and polite youngster had his upper breast pocket full of coins, and as he bent over to give Bevin a hand, the money showered down on the Cabinet officer. The airman grabbed for his pocket —and let loose the hatch cover, which landed on Bevin's head. Two British body-guards grabbed for their guns, but the Foreign Minister merely rubbed his head good naturedly and climbed up into the cockpit.

One visit that meant a lot to the airlift was that of Secretary of the Air Force Stuart Symington, who arrived at Christmas. By this time General LeMay had been replaced by Lieutenant General John Cannon as head of USAFE. There had been some friction between the airlift command and USAFE headquarters even under LeMay. It became much worse under Cannon, who apparently did not have a very high regard for MATS. Under the table of organization that he established, Tunner was not allowed to communicate directly with the commander of MATS in the States, although Tunner was a MATS officer. The airlift was under USAFE, and Cannon required all communications to clear through USAFE headquarters. The inability to pick up a phone and get something done in a hurry hampered the already difficult supply situation.

On Christmas morning General Tunner took Secretary Symington on a tour of Rein-Main. The Secretary saw the appalling living conditions at the base and then visited the maintenance shops. He stopped beside a grimy mechanic who was working on an engine and said, with a politician's charm: "Hello, I'm Stu Symington. Just wanted to see how you're getting along with that engine."

Perhaps the mechanic had never heard of Stu Symington, or he may merely have been disgruntled. In any event he was not daunted by this high-level civilian and replied, "Oh, I'll get it fixed all right, but I could do it better if I had better tools."

"What's the matter with your tools?" asked Symington.

The mechanic held up a pair of pliers, a wrench, and a screw driver. "See these?" he asked. "Well I bought them myself here in Germany, and they're all I got, and I can't get any more, and they ain't worth a good god-damn."

At the end of the tour Symington asked Tunner for a detailed report on the airlift's needs. Tunner's staff worked the rest of Christmas and all the next day turning out a thick document headed "Supply and Maintenance Problem—First Airlift Task Force" that covered every problem from housing to the shortage of shop equipment. The original was placed in Symington's hands—a copy went to USAFE. Symington went directly back to Washington and apparently started to push buttons. Orders came down requisitioning better housing, and construction was immediately begun on emergency barracks. Long needed supplies started to arrive in quantity, accompanied by staff officers from the Pentagon to see what else was needed.

On that same Christmas there was another conflict between airlift command and a USAFE headquarters; the subject was Bob Hope. The comedian was famous for his trips during the war to bring troops of entertainers to foreign military posts. Hope made his last trip in 1946 and then settled down for a much needed rest. In the fall of 1948, Secretary Symington met Hope in Romanoff's restaurant in Hollywood and on the spur of the moment asked him to put on a Christmas show for the airlift. Hope agreed, and the coming show was widely reported in the press of the United States and Germany. *The Task Force Times* was full of it for weeks, and airlift personnel waited avidly for this Christmas entertainment.

Hope arrived in Germany on December 23 with a troop

that included one who had adopted the name of the capital city as his own—Irving Berlin. It was on that day that Tunner learned that the performances were to be held in places where it would be almost impossible for many airlift personnel to see the show. On Christmas Eve, a performance was scheduled in downtown Wiesbaden, far from the air base, but convenient to USAFE headquarters. The second performance on Christmas Day would be held in downtown Berlin, convenient for the occupation troops but inaccessible to all but the few airlift personnel stationed at Templehof. The official record of the Staff conference on December 23 stated: "General Tunner expressed his extreme displeasure over the Bob Hope show, which had been billed as a show for the airlift." An official protest was not possible, but Tunner could, and did, issue an ultimatum to USAFE headquarters immediately—either the shows were to be put on where the airlift personnel could see them or all mention of the airlift was to be dropped from the advance billing and the publicity. Since Hope had come over specifically to entertain the airlift, he surely would have been distressed to learn that they were not to see his shows, and the press would have had a field day. Three more shows were quickly scheduled at airlift bases.

Most of the airlift Christmas celebration was not so acrimonious, and many fliers and crewmen had a fine time playing Santa Claus, complete with whiskers, for Berlin kids. Airlift personnel at Fassberg started "Operation Santa Claus" in which pilots and crewmen wrote home asking their families and friends to collect toys for Berlin children. On Christmas morning 53,000 parcels were flown to Gatow where the most robust member of the outfit played Santa Claus for thousands of children waiting at the field. One squadron had a similar scheme called "Operation Sleigh Bells" which netted 1400 gifts which several of their Santa Clauses distributed in the children's wards of hospitals. An Army Transport unit at Giessen collected 48,000 pounds of assorted candy. Having no plane of their own to fly Santa, and with the autobahn closed to their trucks, they borrowed the personal plane of General Koenig, Commander of the French Forces in Germany.

Many individual pilots who could get the day off visited in Berlin to bring Christmas cheer to children, most of them carrying candy which they had bought themselves or with collections raised by their squadron mates. But the most important Christmas gifts for Berliners were the planes that droned steadily overhead on this day, as on any other, carrying almost 6000 tons of life-giving supplies.

EIGHT

The Victorious City

In the dark, cold winter of 1948–49, there was one group of people in Berlin who were doing well, or at least keeping busy—a horde of self-styled seers. The city was full of soothsayers, clairvoyants, astrologers, card-readers, palmists, phrenologists, and wise women who read the future from coffee grounds and tea leaves. Nobody knew how many there were. Most carried on their mysterious rites under cover, either for fear of the police or to avoid taxes. But there were three small magazines devoted to astrology that circulated more or less regularly when paper to print them was available in the black market, and all newspapers carried astrology columns and ads saying: "What will the year 1949 bring? Scientific astrological predictions; give date of birth."

The avid interest of Berliners in the occult, which amounted for a short time to a mania, was based partly on fear, partly on hope. No one knew what the next day, the next hour, would bring, and reassurance from the stars or cards, or tea leaves fostered a belief that things would become better. Most of the soothsayers were drab, unprepossessing people who barely eked out a living despite their great popularity. There were so many of them

163

that they cut their fees to a few pfennigs as a price war developed.

The Communists, always suspicious, thought that there must be a dark or sinister motive behind the practice of these seers. A Communist newspaper investigated two of them and, sure enough, came up with "proof" that one was working for the British while the other "is engaged in close collaboration with the Americans." It was not clear what the Western powers expected to get out of the activities of these soothsayers, but the Communists were sure that they had some nefarious purpose. "The Strumm police," wrote the Communist paper, "would long ago have taken action against these two principal leaders of the soothsayers' chorus if these two women did not enjoy the favor of the Western occupying forces."

A cause of more concern to the Western military authorities were mystics who preached strange cults. Normally, the cynical and sophisticated Berliners would pay little attention to offbeat proposals—but these were not normal times and the fear of a mystic turning into another fanatical leader was always present. One was a little man named Jakob Kuny who had started a cult of which he said: "My Kunyology preaches love as a totally independent force, like electricity. Today we need something to defeat the atom bombs. Party dogmas will not help; only Kunyology will do it."

When Kuny started to attract large crowds the police, probably at the instigation of the occupation authorities, forbade him to speak. This led to a mass demonstration in front of the Technical High School one evening in which some 5000, mostly young students, blocked the streets lead-

ing to the square and held up traffic. They serenaded Kuny
with cowbells, frying pans, whistles, and other noisemakers
while they chanted: "Down with the police, we want
Kuny's release" or "We don't care what Marshall planned,
if we can't hold our Kuny's hand." It was a mark of the
times that the authorities restrained this funny little man
with a mystic doctrine—but Hitler had started as a funny
little man with a mystic doctrine.

As winter came and Berliners awoke by candlelight in
their icy hovels, life in the city took on more of a surrealistic character. It was a city with two governments, two
kinds of money, two kinds of newspapers, and two radio
stations from which newscasters broadcast diametrically
opposing statements. A city in which people ate their din-
ners at three o'clock in the morning when electricity was
available, a city whose beauty parlors gave permanent
waves at five o'clock in the morning, whose drug stores
sold coal at the back door, and whose coal yards sold meat
at the back gate. It was a city in which not a single taxi
cab moved through the streets.

Not everybody was working. By mid-winter the scarcity
of power had caused widespread unemployment; almost
one-third of the people were on relief. But everybody was
busy—busy with basic things like getting to places without
transportation, searching for necessities in poorly stocked
stores or on the black market, and standing in queues for
endless hours. And Berliners were busy waiting. They
waited, it seemed, for everything. Time was an unwanted
luxury and the bane of their daily lives. An old man standing on a street corner typified the spirit of the waiting. A

friend approached and asked: "Are you waiting for a bus?"

The old man thought about this for a moment, looking skyward. Then he replied: "I'm waiting for the electricity to come on so that I can press my pants. I'm waiting for the tobacco ration to be distributed. I'm waiting for the next currency reform. I'm waiting for Stalin to give up and lift the blockade. And, now that you ask, I guess I'm waiting a little bit for the bus, too."

When later asked to list the hardships of the blockade, a representative sample of Berliners placed lack of electricity first, followed by lack of fuel for heating, and then lack of food or the dullness of the food. In November 1948, however, a public opinion survey placed fuel first and the power shortage second. As winter approached, cold became a personal enemy of every Berliner. There was virtually no coal available for heating homes. The ration for the entire winter for families with no small children was twenty-five pounds. And there was no place to go to get warm. Space heating was limited to hospitals and other institutions caring for the young or aged. Even most schools had no heat. Few Berliners had warm winter clothing to bundle up in. One either tried to keep moving to get warm or huddled, shivering, fully clothed, in bed.

Typical of the caustic humor with which Berliners spoke of the hardships of the blockade were comments such as "I can't freeze, I'm shivering too much." Or the reverse, "I'm freezing more than I can shiver." While there were but few recorded deaths from exposure, many fatalities from pneumonia and other diseases were undoubtedly brought on by the cold. Several people died from going to bed with the gas on. When the flow was turned off the flame went out; when it came back on the sleepers were asphyxiated.

Yet when they were offered an opportunity to be warm, Berliners refused it. The trees in the city's parks and forests were the pride of Berlin, particularly the Grunewald, an extensive woods on the west side of the city. The people had a fondness verging on reverence for their trees. Anticipating an acute fuel shortage during the winter, the occupation authorities ordered the Magistrat, in late October, to cut down enough trees in the "forests, parks, public gardens, streets, and private gardens" to provide 350,000 cubic meters of firewood. This would have meant cutting down at least half of the Grunewald.

The people were horrified. This was nothing short of sacrilege. If it was a choice between freezing and losing their trees, they would freeze. The Magistrat made a counter proposal to cut down only 120,000 feet of timber, which could be done by thinning the forest. The military commanders accepted this for, as General Howley said: "As far as I was concerned, this was a matter for the Germans themselves to decide. Personally, I thought it wiser to cut down the trees and keep warm." Berliners grumbled even at this limited butchery of the trees, which finally resulted in one small box of smoky, damp, firewood for each family just before Christmas that was consumed in a few days.

Russian propaganda made much of the tree cutting incident. It was another proof that the Americans were barbarians who had no aesthetic sense and did not hesitate to blast Berlin's beauty. The city, the Russian radio blared, would be completely denuded of trees if the Americans had their way. This would not only destroy the landscape but would wreck the watershed—and the city would be ten degrees hotter in summer. Although these charges, like most of the Soviet abuse, were directed at the Americans, the tree cutting idea was the brainchild of General Herbert, the British commander in Berlin.

The inconvenience of the blockade was not limited to Berliners. Members of the foreign press corps had their troubles in trying to do their daily work. One American correspondent later wrote: "I knew the Russians were having my house watched to find out who was supplying me with information. It became harder and harder for my tipsters to get in touch with me. For several months I kept three apartments in Berlin in order to make communication easier. My activities were not without risk to my associates, and even to my cook and chauffeur. They could expect to be interrogated, possibly arrested, by the MVD if the Russians ever entered West Berlin.

"But the big dangers—if you believed in them—were not what made the life of a reporter in the cold war so difficult. The main trouble was the trivial nuisances of daily living. To be in my office by nine, my two secretaries would have had to leave their homes at 6:30 in the morning, for hardly any street cars were running, and no buses at all. The subway ran only every twenty minutes and was so unbelievably jammed that, assuming they could get into the cars at all, the two girls would have arrived more dead than alive. And if they left for home at 6 P.M., they would have had to walk all the way, for by afternoon there was no public transportation at all.

"Moreover, they would have had to walk through a pitch

dark city, for there were no street lights either. In order to have my secretaries in shape for work, I therefore had to have them fetched in my car and taken home again. That was not so easy, for our gasoline ration had been severely cut. I also had to give them—as did the other correspondents—at least one warm meal a day or they would have collapsed, for at home they could not cook—there was not enough gas."

One of the major annoyances of life in Berlin during the winter of the blockade was the continuation of the two-currency system of east and west marks. Both currencies were legal tender, but everybody wanted to take in west marks and pay out east marks—an obvious impossibility. Businesses tried to pay workers in east marks and sell their goods for west marks. Increasingly stores refused to sell goods except for west marks and the black market operated entirely on the stronger currency. The licensed exchanges in the west sectors tried to hold the rate of exchange to slightly over four east marks for one west mark but limited the amount that could be exchanged to two marks per person. Those with a surplus of the Soviet-sponsored currency had to resort to unlicensed black-market money changers who were asking as much as nine east marks for one west mark. This situation was corrected in the spring of 1949 when the Western powers, at last giving up the hope of a single currency for Berlin, made the west mark the only legal tender in their sectors of the city.

A situation that was amusing to all but the Soviets developed when the staff and performers of Communist-controlled Radio Berlin demanded that their wages be paid partly in west marks. The irony of this was the fact that the people who were demanding pay in west marks were broadcasting the Communist line that east marks were more valuable than west marks.

Another Communist-inspired radio theme was that the food in West Berlin was of very poor quality compared to that of East Berlin; and the Soviets were most unhappy to learn that some of the people who were doing the broadcasting were buying their food in West Berlin. The democratic newspaper *Tagesspiegel* commented that they were probably eating "the horrible tinned meat, the unhealthy dried potatoes, and the maggot-infested raisins" in order to try and use up the "vanishing" food stocks of West Berlin.

Russian harassment of West Berliners continued, but on a somewhat reduced scale, and it was now meeting greater resistance from both Berliners and the occupation forces. When the Soviets evicted forty known democrats from their houses in the eastern sector, the free press of West Berlin insisted that a like number of Communists be deprived of housing in the west sectors. West Berliners who crossed into the Soviet-controlled sector were still subjected to search and confiscation of their west marks but here, too, resistance was increasing. When an east sector policeman tried to search the baggage of a woman traveling by subway across the east-west sector border, she boxed his ears and was protected from arrest by a threatening crowd of fellow passengers. In several cases Markgraf police were forced to flee before an irate crowd when they attempted their searches. The *Tagesspiegel* added to the discomfiture of the police by blacklisting particular officers with notices such as:

ERWIN WOLF, *Police Sergeant*
of the 11th Police Precinct, Magizinstrasse,
who lives on Gross Hamburgerstrasse, Berlin N4,
is stealing baggage at the Neanderstrasse subway station.

Meanwhile, the Soviet propaganda campaign continued in full swing, directed particularly against the Americans. Its virulence is indicated by an excerpt from a Radio Berlin broadcast: "What has American imperialism to offer us in the way of culture? Is it the boogie-woogie culture and the sensational and immoral films which appeal to the lowest instincts? Is it the poisoning of our youth by the dirty fantasy of Henry Miller and the dirty hands of Jean Paul Sartre? Is it the shameless exploitation of the poverty of our young women which makes them into soldier's prostitutes and infects our girls with American syphilis at the price of a bar of chocolate and a few Camels?"

But the West had now developed counter propaganda. The American Army had started a second radio station in Berlin, RIAS, which broadcast democratic news and countered the Russian inspired libelous broadcasts. In the face of electricity stoppages and the scarcity of radio batteries, RIAS also employed cruising sound trucks to broadcast news at street corners.

Both the free radio and press made much of the reintroduction by the Russians in the east sector of the hated "house warden" system of the Nazis. These house wardens were minor officials who each had responsibility for a single apartment house or group of private houses. They were supposed to assist in matters such as the distribution of ration cards, but their real function was to observe and report any signs of political dissatisfaction. Berliners remembered neighbors and friends who had been hauled off to concentration camps at the instigation of Nazi house-warden informers, and the news that the Communists were adopting the same system served to strengthen their resistance.

In November the Communists introduced a new terror tactic by announcing that the People's Police force was being increased to 400,000 and by bringing strong units of this force into East Berlin. The People's Police was a federal force in East Germany which had initially been recruited from former German soldiers who had been captured and converted to Communism in Russian prison camps.

The force was armed with heavy infantry weapons and was obviously an embryonic army rather than a police force. Their introduction into East Berlin and the rumor that they were to be commanded by some former German generals who had been Russian captives led to the assumption that an invasion of West Berlin was imminent. At the same time, in connection with Russian army maneuvers in East Germany, a ring of tanks were assembled facing Berlin. The Soviets were obviously trying to do all that they could to instill panic in West Berlin and, for a time, the Allied intelligence services were quite nervous—far more nervous than the Berliners who by this time were taking a "wolf, wolf" attitude toward such Soviet tactics. They reasoned that if a real invasion was imminent, the Communist press would not be reporting so freely on its preparation.

The People's Police move was a bluff, but there is reason to believe that the Soviets did plan an actual *putsch* in West Berlin at about the same time. The plan, as reported by several foreign correspondents and the West Berlin press, called for several "spontaneous" demonstrations of the populace of West Berlin, to be fomented by Communist agitators. Small units of the east sector Communist youth organization were to infiltrate the crowds, armed with revolvers, and shoot at the West Berlin police. Allied troops would have to come to the aid of the poorly armed western police, there would be more shooting and perhaps some casualties.

In response to this "massacre," protest demonstrations would then be held in the east sector to demand the liberation of the population of West Berlin from their "imperialist oppressors." In the face of this spontaneous demand, People's Police would occupy German administration buildings in the west sectors to "protect" them. After two or three days of such chaos in West Berlin, the Soviet government would inform the Western powers that it would have to intervene in order to restore order in West Berlin.

News of this plan reached several foreign correspondents—who all had paid informers in East Berlin—at about the same time. They reported it in dispatches as a rumor. West Berlin newspapers learned from their sources that a list of Socialist Unity leaders living in the west sectors had been drawn up so that they might be protected from "the terror measures of the allies in case of disturbances." Also it was learned that the Markgraf police were distributing small arms to the Communist youth organization. No one knows at what level this "conquest of Berlin" was planned, but it was called off when the press raised the alarm.

During the late fall and early winter, the blockade ring was tightened around Berlin, with more checkpoints established to prevent smuggling. New blockade restrictions were announced in the Communist press almost daily. Controls were extended to the subway lines running between the east and west sectors, and more and more Soviet and East German border guards were called up to man at least seventy-five checkpoints on the east-west boundaries of the city. Still, smuggling continued and much food and other materials moved from east to west by means of smugglers. East zone farmers, avid for west marks, found many devious ways to circumvent border guards. Stolid, seeming innocent, peasant women boarded elevated trains at their farthest terminals in the suburbs with butter, eggs, and fresh fowls hidden under their voluminous skirts. Children carried bags that might have contained school books but that actually held farm-fresh food.

Outwitting the east sector police became a matter of personal pride to many West Berliners intent on securing coal or other supplies. Seemingly innocent housewives sneaked shopping bags containing drugs and medicines past the guards into the eastern sector to trade these commodities, scarce in East Berlin, for food and fuel.

The frustrated Markgraf police dug ditches and erected barricades to funnel this flow of traffic through their checkpoints, but their efforts were largely ineffective. Several *hinterhauser* (sprawling apartment houses linked together with courtyards and passageways) extended on both sides of the sector boundaries. One could enter such houses in the Soviet sector and come out in the western sectors, and the police obviously could not patrol every hallway.

On a larger scale, produce was smuggled in from West Germany by the truckload. A widespread and efficient illicit trucking business flourished, based on bribery and forged papers. Trucks from beyond the Elbe passed the checkpoint at Helmstedt by exhibiting papers showing that the cargo was consigned to a firm in the east zone. Once safely inside the guard ring around Berlin they switched papers to exhibit a pass into the western sectors.

General Howley reported that a German came to his office one day with an offer: "General," he said, "if you will provide me with the necessary trucks and ask no questions I'll bring any quantity of food that you want into Berlin. It's all a question of knowing the way."

Howley inferred that he meant that it was a matter of knowing whom to pay off, but he could not take advantage of the offer. In general, said Howley, the authorities officially denounced this smuggling but actually closed their eyes to it. If things got really bad they might need the smugglers. There was also a minor amount of smuggling on the airlift. Some pilots made a little money on the side by carrying cartons of cigarettes, pounds of coffee, and bottles of brandy which they could readily dispose of at fancy prices at Templehof.

Mobility was an absolute prerequisite for smuggling, and an active market in credentials that permitted interzone movement came into being. Interzone passes were free in West Germany for those who were entitled to them. Flight cards, which were necessary before one could book passage from the west to the east, cost about 150 marks. In the summer of 1948, a pass and a card could be illicitly obtained for about 400 west marks. By the end of October the price had risen to about 6000 marks.

By winter the black market was better organized. There was less evidence of it in the streets but in the eastern sector special stores, which were open to West Berliners, were openly dealing in black-market goods. These were presumably owned by nationals of Russian satellite countries —Bulgarians, Hungarians, Poles, and Yugoslavs—but they obviously could not operate without the protection of highly placed Russians. They sold food, textiles, cigarettes, and all kinds of luxuries at usurious prices. The Yugoslavs specialized in cigarettes and manufactured millions of fake Camels, Lucky Strikes, and Chesterfields that were packaged to so closely imitate the American product that only the most critical inspection would disclose the deception, although the difference in quality was apparent on the first puff. They also had some real American cigarettes that had come to Yugoslavia via UNRAA and had been smuggled from there to Berlin.

One day the Soviets cracked down on the Yugoslavs, either because their behind-the-scenes Russian patron had lost favor or because of political differences with the mother country. The police confiscated millions of cigarettes and threw them on the market at two east marks per pack, for the bogus brands. In the two-currency economy, cigarettes were still a medium of exchange on the black market, and when the Russians released a flood of them, the price of a pack of genuine American cigarettes dropped to five west marks. This wreaked havoc with black-market economics. All prices spiraled madly downward, and many black-market operators were wiped out.

A statistical picture of Berlin during the blockade had some surprising facets. Despite the dull food, fuel shortages, electrical stoppages, lack of transportation, unemployment, and the dual currency, the basic functions of life continued very much as they had before the blockade. There was virtually no change in the number of marriages or the rate of divorce. The birth rate sank very slightly during the nine months after the blockade was lifted, but the decline was insignificant.

Although street lighting would seem to encourage burglary, crimes such as robbery and house breaking declined during the blockade. Some police experts reported that crime in West Berlin was less than in any other population group of the same size in the Western world. Disease, as measured by the number of people in hospitals, did not increase, and serious diseases such as tuberculosis, typhoid, and diphtheria declined. The death rate showed a moderate increase, particularly among the very young.

In short, life in Berlin was hard but not unbearable. Its most prominent aspects were drabness and the difficulties surrounding even routine household functions, and these caused psychological rather than physical hardships. As the days got shorter people were oppressed by the continual, dreary darkness which prevented them from reading or relaxing in other ways during the long winter evenings, and most people went to bed early, exhausted by their grim existences.

But in spite of the blockade, life in West Berlin seemed to be more desirable than life in East Berlin to most of

the inhabitants of the city. Newspaper advertisements by
East Berliners who wanted to move to the west sectors of
the city were not uncommon: "Will exchange two-room
apartment in east sector for one or two-room apartment in
west sector," or "Seeking two or three-room apartment in
west sector in exchange for unusually fine apartment in
Prenzlauer Berg [east sector]. All glass intact, sixty marks
monthly," or "Exchange 2½-room apartment east sector
for one-room apartment British or American sector." There
were few, if any, ads from people in the west sectors who
wanted to move in with the Communists.

On the plus side was the Berliners' sense of humor, their
ability to joke about their misfortunes. This had always
been characteristic of Berliners and during the blockade
it stood them in good stead. A British diplomat, returning
to Berlin after an absence of years, commented: "The
character of the Berliners has not altered. There was the
same grim humor, the same sense of detachment, the same
skepticism, the same dogged obstinacy. It may well be
that Germany will regain her confidence through the per-
sistence of the curious character, sardonic, and yet individual, which that huge, amorphous Babylon has evolved
for itself within the space of sixty years."

The total attitude of Berliners toward the blockade
might be summed up in one quip: "God knows, even the
best blockade is no bargain. But if there must be a blockade, then it's better to be blockaded by the Soviets and
fed by the Americans. Just imagine if it were the other
way round."

Their hardships and their uniform resistance to the
Russians created in Berliners a solidarity that had not

existed before the blockade. A manifestation of this was the increase in visiting, which was for many the only available form of relaxation. Recreational activities existed, on a limited scale, but getting to them was difficult without transportation. Movie attendance was off more than 50 percent, and a darkened café with ersatz coffee was not a great attraction. In some of the formerly gay night spots, bar girls listlessly talked to each other while the few customers tried to read newspapers by dim candlelight. Some cultural activities continued despite the difficulties. The Berlin Philharmonic Orchestra held concerts regularly under the batons of several world famous visiting conductors, and visiting artists and musicians performed frequently by candlelight. Outdoor concerts were given in the Olympic Stadium, and a Shakespeare company performed in an open air theatre.

But the main scene of relaxation for most Berliners was a neighbor's kitchen, the only room in the house which might be heated. If one household had fuel while others did not, the neighbors were naturally invited over to get warm. One man wrote somewhat testily: "There were parliaments of nine women in my kitchen, which was so small that it was crowded when only two people were in it." Those who had a source of light were popular and willingly shared their illumination with all who could crowd in. One fortunate woman who lived near the Templehof elevated station was hooked in to the transit power lines, which came from the east zone. She had light all the time and recalled:

"So, every evening, my lamp served all our acquaintances and neighbors. This source of light helped to solve those countless problems which, especially for those with jobs, the blockade with its electrical stoppages made almost impossible to overcome. For one came running home from the office into a dark apartment. By candlelight one could get something to eat all right, but to darn stockings was almost impossible—although it was even more impossible to wear stockings with holes in them to the office. . . . So people wrote political articles, did their school work, knitted clothes for the baby in my apartment—everyone who needed light came to me."

Family and small neighborhood groups were bound together by stronger ties than ever before. A few years later a sixty-one-year-old professional man remembered: "How was it during the time of the Berlin blockade? In the evening we sat together in a group with several people who lived in the same building . . . and talked over what had happened during the day. . . . There were thick clouds of smoke from half filled pipes or from home-made cigarettes made from tobacco we had grown ourselves, glasses of thin beer or some artificial mixture, and now and then the inevitable corn liquor from some dark source. In the middle of the circle was a very old candle or taper of tremendous size, with a thick, lumpy wick. . . . Jokes and songs always came into their own, and the airlift planes roaring through the night sang the bass in perfect time. . . .

"The unity among those who lived in the building often reminded one of the sociability of the air-raid shelters several years before, but without the horribly oppressive worry about the family members in the battle far way and about one's own danger in the emergency bunkers. We would stay together cheerfully until almost 11 o'clock. The tiny light in the radio, which was already turned on, lighted up punctually [when the current came on], and all sharpened their ears to hear the evening broadcast. The electric light shone wonderfully bright, even though we had only half the bulbs on for the sake of economy. The candle, of which we were so proud, was blown out with huge puffs, and the evening magic was over. We quickly parted, in order to make preparations for the next day, and immediately went to bed, since electricity had to be saved for the even more necessary cooking purposes."

As a result of this solidarity, morale became institutionalized. A certain standard of conduct was expected of one and maintained by collective example or pressure. Many people might have been far more discouraged by their personal experiences had not their morale been sustained by the attitude of the group. Society became a stabilizing force that made it less likely for the individual to succumb to the hardships of pressures in his own life.

Another factor that played a large part in the final victory of Berlin was pride—the pride of the people in themselves and particularly, as time went on, a pride in being accepted as full partners of the Western Allies and pride at being recognized and lauded by the outside world. There had been a feeling of rejection caused by the lost war, by three years of austerity, cold and hunger in a destroyed city, and by the stern occupation policies. Then, almost overnight, Berliners ceased to feel and be treated as a conquered people. Their former enemies not only helped them at great expense and risk but—more important—they praised them. To many Berliners the hardships of the

blockade were more than compensated for by this acceptance by the Allies and the outside world.

In an essay contest held after the blockade by a newspaper, *Der Abend,* many of the writers expressed some
such thought as, "the world respected us," "the world was
watching us," "the world cared about us." This was a grati-
fying experience, and some found themselves almost embarrassed by it, like the housewife who wrote:

"Since the Western powers up until the time of the
blockade had treated us Berliners, and all other Germans,
as third- or even fourth-class citizens, I was convinced that
for the sake of Berlin, they would never engage in open
conflict. I was greatly surprised that they kept up the airlift . . . for such a long time. But I was even more amazed
at the almost affectionate recognition that they gave to the
behavior of us Berliners during the blockade. This recognition was a little embarrassing to me, since I did not regard myself at all as a heroine, but much rather as a miser-
able, half-starved little 'sausage' for whom in this situation there was no other choice but to hold out."

Another housewife felt that this knowledge of being
noticed and respected put even the most routine tasks on
a high moral plane. She wrote: "The world, the press, the
speeches of our city fathers, letters from outside Berlin—
they all spoke of the bravery of our conduct. The Berlin
housewives were accorded particularly high praise. Many
times I have had to do things that were unpleasant, and I
often had to do my part of difficult tasks, but unfortunately
there was rarely anybody there to bestow appropriate attention on me. But now, even if together with a large
group, I was given this satisfaction, I was a heroine! A

Berlin housewife who kept her ears stiff as iron, who did her duty as a matter of course. Of course I was not entirely at ease when all this attention came my way. Things were made so easy for us. We just felt ourselves to be part of the West and acted accordingly. Nevertheless, this extra praise helped to give a stiff backbone, and I walked proudly through the streets. I was helping to write a proud page in the history of Berlin's housewives."

A public opinion surveyor summarized this mixture of pride and embarrassment that marked the collective attitude of Berliners during the winter of the blockade: "Berliners themselves made fun of the boastfulness which, to some degree, was implicit in their own behavior. They smiled when some leading personality of the West spoke over the radio and praised the courage and steadfastness of the Berliners. But in this smile there was something akin to embarrassment and pride. We didn't know whether we were really 'heroes' or not. And if we are 'heroes,' it isn't because we have done so much. In the last analysis, we are heroes because we are afraid of the Soviets and because we happen to live in Berlin."

Under the Berlin constitution, elections to the City Assembly were to take place every two years. The first election had been held in October 1946. A new election was due to be held in the fall of 1948. Plans for this had been under way before the Assembly had been driven from the City Hall in the Soviet sector in September. After it moved to the British sector, the municipal government finalized these plans for an election on December 5. The Communist-controlled Socialist Unity Party promptly announced that it would boycott the elections, and in reply to a letter from the city government, Kotikov made it clear that the only conditions under which the Russians would permit a city-wide election amounted to nothing short of Western capitulation to Soviet demands for control of the entire city. The election, therefore, would be held only in the western sectors and would formalize the split of the city into completely separate sections.

The Communists, through the Socialist Unity Party, made strenuous efforts to interfere with the pre-election activities of the democratic parties. Party workers were kidnapped by east sector police and dragged into Soviet territory. Socialist Unity squads shouted Communist slogans at democratic party meetings, hurled stink bombs, occupied halls in which meetings were to be held, and otherwise terrorized political meetings in the western sectors.

There was a difference, however, between this and the previous election. The Communists now found themselves facing democratic action squads composed of heavily muscled young trade unionists who were more anxious for a fight than the easterners. Fist fights preceded many meetings and on at least one occasion the Social Democrats set up a first-aid station outside a meeting hall where the Communist hecklers were treated after they were thrown out.

The Communist propaganda campaign was aimed at convincing West Berliners that they should stay away from the polls in an election which, said the Communists, would irrevocably split the city. Besides, they said, it was useless to vote because the elections were fraudulent, and the results that would be announced were already reposing in the files of the American Military Government. The election was a device of the American generals who wanted to continue the tension in Berlin for their own ends and retain control of the city in order to exploit the workers. A special appeal was made to women with newspaper items such as this addressed to:

> HOUSEWIVES IN THE WEST—
> Do you want to indicate by voting that you approve of the present conditions? Do you want people to think that you are satisfied with electricity rationing, with the tiny gas ration, with the dark and cold homes into which the rain still comes, with the eternal canned food, and with all the difficulties brought on by the west marks? On December 5, get even with those who want to split Berlin. Don't vote.

A radio jingle followed the same theme:

> Don't be lured by promises sweet.
> Think of the dried potatoes you've had to eat.
> Think of all the cut down trees
> And the dark, cold rooms in which you freeze.
> Don't vote for the candidates, like a dunce,
> Whose parties have already betrayed you once.

(The translator of the above gibberish apologized by saying that if his work seemed crude it really was a faithful rendition of the original German.)

The Communists also injected their favorite terror tactics. The movement of the People's Police into Berlin and the massing of tanks coincided with the election campaign. Starting December 1, all leaves for east sector police were canceled. When General Howley announced that there were sufficient Allied troops available to protect the western sectors from east zone police or armed Communist mobs, the eastern press interpreted this as a move to reinforce West Berlin by writing stories with such headlines as "Weapons Over the Airlift—Remarkable Election Preparations for Berlin's West Sectors." The usual claims that the Allies were preparing to leave Berlin after the elections were based, this time, on a supposed leak from London.

When election day dawned there was some apprehension in West Berlin that East German police or even Red Army troops might intervene at the last minute. The armed forces of the Western powers were held in readiness, and reinforced west sector police patrolled the city and were massed near the polling places. There were only a few minor incidents, in which armed Russian soldiers appeared at outlying polling places, but they left in the face of superior Western forces.

Despite all attempts at intimidation, West Berliners went to the polls in droves. Almost 87 percent of the 1,500,000 eligible voters cast ballots, a far higher percentage than is ever achieved in any American election. The Social Democrats won an absolute majority with 64.5 percent, the other two democratic parties splitting the balance. The U.S. Military Government calculated that the strength of the Communist-inspired Socialist Unity Party had shrunk from 14 percent in the 1946 election to 5 percent in 1948.

After the election, the initiative in Berlin began to pass from the east to the west. Indicative of this was the tightening of a counter blockade that had, up to that time, been of a partial and sporadic nature. Anyone had been free to buy anything in the French and British sectors and carry it into Soviet controlled territory without hindrance, and there were only minor restrictions in the American sector.

In January 1949, this changed as vehicles bound to or from East Germany were forbidden to cross the American and British zones. By this time the economy of West Germany was well along the comeback road. East Germany had vital need of many raw materials from the west. The exact extent to which the counter blockade hampered the East German economy is not known, but many eastern zone factories were forced to lay off workers or curtail working hours because of it.

In cases where the Soviets were permitted to buy in West Berlin, they were required to pay in west marks, which they usually refused to do since they did not recognize this as legal tender. On one occasion a member of Kotikov's staff approached Howley's office to plead for special consideration. Moscow had ordained that a great memorial to the Russian dead in the battle for Berlin be erected in the city. Built largely of pink marble ripped from Hitler's Chancellory, this was to be decorated with twenty-five tons of bronze wreaths and plaques and a large statue of Lenin. When they were ready for the bronze, the West Berlin company that had cast it refused delivery unless payment was made in west marks. Please, said the Russians, would not Howley intervene? Nothing had been said about west marks when the order was placed. Howley would not intervene and the Russians had to scrape up 185,000 west marks to get their decorations. Two weeks later they were back with a more important problem. Another company that had made Lenin's head also demanded west marks. The Russians had to deliver this hated currency before they could take home the head of their hero.

Meanwhile, the airlift continued to drone steadily overhead. When the weather moderated in January it was apparent that the airlift had the blockade licked. It was now operating with its full force of 225 American C-54s and about 150 assorted British planes. On days of good weather it approached its theoretical maximum goal of landing a plane every three minutes at each of the three airports every hour of the twenty-four. Tonnage was approaching a figure of 8000 tons a day, which would be realized in early spring.

On February 18, Secretary of State Dean Acheson sent a telegram to General Clay: "I extend to you our Government's heartiest congratulations for communication to all who have been associated with this great cooperative enterprise." The occasion was the arrival in Berlin of the one millionth ton of airlifted supplies. The Secretary added: "The success of the airlift has enabled the Western powers to maintain their rights and discharge their obligations in Berlin as prescribed by solemn international agreement and has given encouragement to the efforts of the democratic peoples of Europe to resist the use of lawless force."

Perhaps the highest commendation of the airlift, albeit unintentional, came from the Soviet officer at the Berlin Air Safety Center who complained that there were so many British and American planes in the corridors that he could not keep track of them. This safety center was one of two activities in Berlin in which four-power participation did not break down. The Russians quietly kept their representatives on it throughout the blockade—probably to learn as much as they could about Western practices in this area. The other activity in which the four powers peacefully continued to share responsibility was the prison that housed the seven war criminals whose lives had been spared at the Nuremberg trials. The guards and administration staff rotated every month among the four powers, and every fourth month throughout the blockade, the Russians provided a staff for this prison and formally and politely took over from one of the Western powers.

The airlift now had the capacity to carry more than the basic necessities of food, fuel, and medical supplies. One day Berliners were delighted to find jam on the shelves of food stores. A wider variety of food became available, particularly cheese. The lift had always carried a minimum quantity of newsprint in 500-pound rolls specially made in Sweden. Berlin's ten free dailies never missed an issue during the blockade. Now the quota of paper was increased to permit the printing of books. Construction materials formed the cargoes of some planes. In the first week of April more than 100 tons of building materials were flown in, including glass, cement, and tools. Five thousand tons of machinery were flown in to get the western sector power plant that had been stripped by the Russians back in operation. A moderate amount of material for industrial production also formed part of the expanded cargoes.

The airlift was now becoming a two-way street. Many planes no longer left Berlin empty. They carried loads of goods manufactured in Berlin to the outside world—perhaps more for propaganda than for profit. In January more than 1,500,000 electric bulbs were exported in crates marked "Made in Blockaded Berlin." A few small electric locomotives made in Berlin and flown out in the C-74 for use in the Ruhr coal mines were the basis of a news story that Berlin was making the locomotives to mine the coal that was flown back into Berlin. In what amounted to a gesture of bravado, five planes were diverted from their normal activity to fly the exhibits of 120 Berlin manufacturing firms to a trade fair in Hanover. Despite the blockade, Berlin was back in business.

The increased beat of the airlift had much to do with the morale of Berliners. Because they considered it their airlift, it was part of their pride. They had the feeling that if they did less, they would be letting the airlift down. Wrote one: "We did not think that our behavior was so remarkable. It was a matter of course to us that we had to hold out. Only in that way could we force those who were blockading us to change their tune. Or did one think that we should betray the airlift pilots, who were helping us without interruption, trusting in our steadfast behavior."

Watching the planes come in and reading the daily tonnage figures became, increasingly, a part of Berlin life. A seventeen-year-old student wrote that the airlift was always the first subject of discussion and the most important news in the paper.

Another recalled: "Often one could see in the subway or elevated that people were happy and relieved when the airlift had broken another record. Similarly, they were disappointed and downcast when, because of bad weather or for some other reason, the tonnage figures sank for a few days. I think that was the case not so much out of fear that supplies might not be adequate, but much more because of the feeling that 'the others over there,' the Russians, would be rubbing their hands and finding support for their eternally repeated theme that the airlift would never be able to bring in enough."

The airlift was omnipresent. It was impressive in the sense that a great waterfall or a majestic mountain is impressive, and it had a symbolic significance that far transcended its mundane purpose of transporting supplies. Virtually all of the essayists who wrote about it after the crisis was over approached their tasks with an emotional reaction that was reflected in superlatives. Others showed their deep feelings in the almost lyrical quality of their descriptions, of which the following passage is an example:

"Every two minutes a plane arrives from West Germany, loaded with food for West Berlin! The sound of engines can be heard constantly in the air, and it is the most beautiful music to our ears. One could stand for hours on the Templehof elevated station platform and watch the silver birds landing and taking off. And at night the brightly illuminated airfield with its countless little colored lights is like something out of a fantasy. It is a wonderful sight, which I shall never forget!"

Berliners who worked at the airfields took particular pride in the airlift because they felt that they were making a personal contribution to it. The number of these people varied, but at the highest point totaled approximately 30,000 who were employed in construction, administration, maintenance, or transportation. Most of these German airlift workers had come from other professions and trades, usually from vocations that were a cut above the work that they were doing at the airfields. But this did not affect their morale or the wholehearted effort they put into making the airlift a success. One supervisor recalled:

"We worked in three shifts, but quite often men would not be able to finish their work before the end of one shift and would voluntarily stay on extra time in order to complete the job. Morale was excellent. In spite of the fact that public transportation was operating only very spasmodically, and many of the men had to walk for more than an hour to work, they were seldom late.... In general, holidays were simply disregarded. If there was work to do, the men came."

The steadily mounting tonnage had a dual effect on American and British personnel. There was a feeling of pride, of course, but a certain complacency was also beginning to make itself evident. The lift was carrying far more than the increased quota that had been established in the fall. The problem was licked, the boys could rest on their laurels. General Tunner felt that things were going too well: "It was necessary, I felt, to do something to shake up the command. But what?"

The answer lay in the spirit of competition that had first been invoked to improve airlift morale. On the Hump airlift, Air Force Day had been celebrated with one big Gung-ho day when the lift went all out for a tonnage record and carried over 5300 tons of gasoline over the Himalayas in a single day. A one day Derby for the Berlin Airlift had also set a record on Air Force Day in September. Looking for something to celebrate, the staff realized that Easter Sunday was but a few days away. The airlift would

have an Easter Parade in the sky, its planes would be mechanical Easter bunnies bringing more than they had ever
carried before to Berlin.

Officially, the plan was a secret. Ten thousand tons were
set as a goal, but the squadrons were not told this. On the
morning of the Saturday before Easter, sergeants from each
squadron operations posted a squadron quota on the "How-
gozit" boards that drew skeptical whistles from the men.
Scuttlebutt quickly brought about a comparison of figures,
and all realized that they added up to a new tonnage record. It was decided that a uniform cargo would be easier
to handle, and coal was selected. Stockpiles of well over
10,000 tons were built up. Maintenance was pressured to
have every possible plane ready to take to the air.

The parade started at noon on Saturday. Everybody
knew that something was in the air and even the D.P.s who
were loading coal heaved their sacks with extra spirit.
Chair borne commandos from headquarters were on the
line to do some flying with the regular crews. As soon as
things were well under way, Tunner flew to Berlin to
watch the planes come in. The excitement was obvious
from the carefree way that the pilots announced themselves
to the tower. This had always amazed the British, but today they were in especially rare form. Plane 5555 was
known as the "cheerful earful" because its pilots competed
to find quaint names for their ship. Sometimes number
5555 was "four nickels," or "two dimes" or "four fivers."
Today the pilot piped out, "Here comes small change on
the range." The pilot of number 77 sometimes referred to
himself as "a bundle from heaven." Today he went all the

way and called out: "Here comes 77, a bundle from heaven, with a cargo of coal for the daily goal."

There was always a special competition between the English bases at Celle and Fassberg. When General Tunner visited Celle, he found that it was running 12 percent ahead of quota. Then he flew to Fassberg where the commander proudly announced that they were 10 percent ahead of schedule. "Fine, fine," said Tunner, "you're doing almost as good as Celle. They're really on the ball over there." The commander dashed for the line, wildly waving his whip.

Shortly after dawn on Sunday morning, the 10,000-ton quota was reached and passed, with several hours to go and the sun rising in a cloudless sky. General Clay sent congratulations to General Tunner on whatever he was doing, and then asked him what the hell it was. Tunner replied that it was an Easter present for Berlin. As the noon hour approached and there was time for only one more plane, somebody ran up to the last ship with a bucket of red paint and in large letters inscribed on its side: "Tons— 12,941, FLIGHTS—1,398."

There are 1,440 minutes in a day. The airlift had come close to averaging one round trip for every minute. The Army Transport Office figured out that the coal they carried was the equivalent of 600 full railroad cars, equal to twelve fifty-car freight trains. And it had been done without a single accident or injury.

Thereafter, the airlift never fell below 9000 tons a day. Tunner claimed that it was the Easter Parade that broke the back of the Berlin blockade by making it clear to the Russians that the city could, if necessary, be maintained on a normal basis without ground transportation. Actually, there had been indications as early as January that the Soviets were beginning to weaken. Certainly, one factor was that the airlift had been able to function through the two worst months of weather and was now rapidly increasing its tonnage. The December elections, in which West Berliners had so decisively repudiated Communism, was another. And a third was surely the effect the counter blockade was having on the East German economy.

The first hint that the blockade was nearing its end came in an interview that the European manager of the International News Service had with Russian Premier Josef Stalin. In reply to a question as to whether the Soviet Union would lift the blockade if the Allies agreed to postpone the establishment of a separate West German State, the Russian dictator replied: "The Soviet Union sees no obstacles to lifting transport restrictions, on the understanding, however, that transport and trade restrictions introduced by the three powers should be lifted simultaneously." There was no reference to the currency situation or any of the other conditions that Russia had been demanding for the previous year.

The actual negotiations, which started on March 15, were between the United States Ambassador to the United Nations, Philip Jessup, and the Soviet representative on the Security Council, Jacob Malik. Russia wanted a meeting of the Council of Foreign Ministers to discuss the whole German problem. Dr. Jessup intimated that no such meeting would be possible while the blockade was in effect.

After consulting with Moscow, Malik replied that, if a

definite date was set for a meeting of the Council of Foreign Ministers, restrictions of trade and transportation in
Berlin could be lifted in advance of the meeting. On May
5, an official statement was issued in Washington, London,
Moscow, and Paris, the first paragraph of which said, "All
restrictions imposed since March 1, 1948, by the Government of the Union of Soviet Socialist Republics on communications, transportation, and trade between Berlin and
the western zones of Germany and between the Eastern
zone and the western zones will be removed on May 12,
1949."

At midnight on May 11, the checkpoint on the autobahn
at the edge of West Berlin looked like New York's Times
Square on New Year's Eve or the Champs Elysées in Paris
on July 14. People, many of them in evening dress, danced
in the road lighted by automobile headlights as the great
crowd waited for the first cars and trucks to reach Berlin.
It was something of a disappointment to the Germans when
the first vehicle turned out to be a carload of American
newsmen, but they were soon followed by the first of a line
of flower-bedecked trucks.

Next day schools were closed, there were mass meetings
with speeches and everybody went on a buying spree that
lasted for days. The two greatest things in West Berlin
were eating and flicking the light switch on and off to
marvel at the electricity. A wonderful part of it was that
prices tumbled. Wholesalers in West Germany were ship-
ping everything transportable to the capital, with the result that coffee selling for thirteen marks in Hamburg
could be bought for ten marks in West Berlin and other
things in proportion. Black marketeers who had thrived

for years were promptly put out of business. However, doctors could not keep up with the demands of patients who suffered from the effects of the sin of gluttony.

And through it all, the airlift planes continued to drone overhead. It would seem as though everyone had forgotten to tell the airlift that the blockade was over. The faith in the Russians that had guided Allied policy so long, had changed to such extreme distrust that the airlift was kept going just in case. Howley wanted 300,000 tons of food and coal stockpiled before the lift stopped. The month after the blockade was over was actually the airlift's biggest month, and it did not completely phase out until September.

Throughout all of the celebrations tributes were paid to the pilots of the airlift and to those who had died in the endeavor. The *Tagesspiegel* devoted a large portion of its front page to a picture of a wrecked plane and reminded its readers that seven British and seventeen American planes had been lost and added: "The lives of forty-eight men weigh heavily in the scales of freedom. And when in a few days the foreign ministers meet in Paris, they will not be permitted to forget these men who made the supreme sacrifice in the battle for democratic rights."

There is some discrepancy in figures on the fatalities of the airlift. The *Tagesspiegel* figure of forty-eight may have been their count of men lost in actual crashes. General Tunner said that the total deaths were seventy-one, most of which were on the ground. The figure most commonly given is seventy-nine, of which thirty-one were American, thirty-nine British, and nine German. Regardless of which figure is accepted, the airlift was the safest air operation in history, considering the number of landings and take-offs involved. There were a total of 276,926 flights to and from Berlin which carried 2,323,067 tons of supplies to the blockaded city.

There is also some difference of opinion as to the cost of the airlift, which *Fortune* described as a "Rolls Royce delivery service to the world's biggest poor house." The Air Force published a figure of $228,738,640 to which the Army added $5,148,984. Under these figures, a ton of coal that cost $15 would have cost $175 to transport. Tunner claimed that the figures were too high, but some civilian experts claimed that they were too low, not allowing nearly enough for depreciation of the planes.

Whatever it cost, no one today disputes that the airlift was worth every penny. At the time there were many on both sides of the Atlantic who could not understand why, after doing their best to pulverize Berlin with bombs, the British and Americans should turn around and do their best to save it. What was so important about this ruined city full of people who had been enemies of the Western democracies? Why should we spend hundreds of millions of dollars and the lives of young men helping these erstwhile enemies? Fortunately, at long last, America's leaders realized that failure to stand fast in Berlin would be to surrender Europe to Communism. The city itself was merely a symbol. By protecting it from Communist conquest, the Anglo-Americans assured the rest of Europe that their promises of freedom and democracy were not empty words.

But the obligation to save Berlin was not entirely political. There was a higher moral commitment. At the

Nuremberg trials the Western powers had indicted the mass of Germans because they failed to fight Nazi tyranny. They would accept no expedient excuses. The German people, said their judges, should have staunchly resisted Hitler and all that he stood for. In Berlin these same judges were in a similar situation. To bow to Communist tyranny would have been to yield to the same weakness for which they had so recently condemned the Germans.

At the time, *Life* magazine editorialized: "Surrender would be a confession that in July 1945, we really did not have the dignity and moral purpose we boasted. It would be a confession that we merely had a gun. We had more than that. We carried with us the integrity of the West. We may have to prove it again in Berlin." The bridge we built in the sky *did* prove it.

Reference Sources
and Acknowledgments

The sources of material used in the preparation of this volume may be broadly divided into three categories: the press, newspapers, and magazines, of the period; official documents and records; specialized reports and memoirs, mostly published in book form.

Day to day newspaper accounts, magazine articles and dispatches from foreign correspondents from the spring of 1945 until the fall of 1949 contained information that was used throughout the book. The outstanding newspaper source in the United States was the *New York Times* and in England, the *London Times* and the *Manchester Guardian*. In Berlin the most helpful newspapers were *Der Abend* and *Tagesspiegel*. Magazines included *Time, Life, Newsweek,* and *U.S. News and World Report*. Among the official documents that were generally helpful were the *State Department Bulletin; Official Gazette of the Control Council of Germany; Germany, 1947–1949—The Story in Documents* (Department of State Publication 3556); *British Zone Review;* and the *Military Government Information Bulletin*.

CHAPTER ONE

Of special interest in connection with this chapter, which is concerned with the situation in Berlin from the beginning of the occupation in 1945 to the beginning of the blockade in June 1948, are the memoirs of the two principal Americans who were involved. Those of General Clay were published under the title *Decision in Germany*, by Lucius Clay, Doubleday & Co., New York, 1950. General Howley's memoirs were titled *Berlin Command*, by Frank Howley, G. P. Putnam's Sons, New York, 1950. Also of value were "The Occupation of Germany," by Philip E. Mosely; *Foreign Affairs*, July 1950; "Soviet Policy in Germany," by Franz Neumann; *Annals of the American Academy of Political and Social Sciences*, May 1949; and *Berlin Sector: A Four Year Report, July 1st, 1945–September 1st, 1949*, Office of Military Government, U.S. Sector, Berlin.

CHAPTERS TWO AND THREE

These chapters deal with the organization of the airlift and its operation through the summer of 1948. During this period, there were many special reports and articles by foreign correspondents in the press. One by Quentin Reynolds in *Collier's* is quoted in the text. There were also numerous articles in *Flying* and *Aviation Weekly*. An article of special interest was "The Berlin Airlift," by C. J. V. Murphy in *Fortune*, November 1948. Another was "One Year of the Berlin Airlift," *Fighting Forces*, August 1949.

A special issue of *The Bee Hive*, the quarterly house organ of United Aircraft Corporation, written by Paul W. Fisher, was titled "Berlin Airlift." A special issue of *Aviations Operation Magazine*, entitled "A Special Study of Operation Vittles" was published in April 1949. *Berlin Airlift—a USAFE Summary* was issued by Headquarters, U.S. Air Force, Europe, in 1949.

These last four sources also contained valuable background material for chapters five to seven.

CHAPTERS FOUR AND EIGHT

These chapters deal with life in Berlin during the blockade. Principal special sources for this material, in addition to the general sources already mentioned, were several books, including General Howley's *Berlin Command.* Others of particular interest were the *Berlin Blockade,* written for the Rand Corporation by W. Phillips Davison and published by Princeton University Press, Princeton, N.J.; *The Berlin Story,* by Curt Riess, Dial Press, New York, 1952; *Berlin Bastion,* by Friedrich Rudl, Frankfurt, 1951. Interesting material was also contained in a series of special dispatches published in *The New Yorker* during the time of the blockade and *Notes on the Blockade of Berlin,* issued by the Control Commission of Germany (British Element), February 1949.

CHAPTERS FIVE, SIX AND SEVEN

These chapters deal with the operation of the airlift after its early "shakedown" period. An important source for these chapters was the memoirs of General Tunner, the man who ran the airlift during this period, which were published under the title *Over the Hump,* by William H. Tunner, Duell, Sloan and Pearce, New York, 1964. Background for much of the material on routine operations, weather, maintenance, communications, and control, etc., was well presented in "A Special Study of Operation Vittles," and the special issue of *The Bee Hive* already mentioned. Many of the anecdotes and special events were the subjects of reports by correspondents and articles in the general news magazines.

CHAPTER EIGHT

Most of the sources mentioned in connection with chapters one and four were also applicable to this chapter. Of special interest was an essay contest held by the Berlin newspaper *Der Abend,* in January 1952, which was announced under the headline: "What do you Remember About the Airlift?" The 342 essays submitted to this contest contained many of the anecdotes and stories of life in the city during the blockade that are presented in this chapter and chapter four.

Acknowledgment must be made to various divisions of the Department of Defense for assistance in the preparation of this volume. These include the Air Force, the Office of the Assistant Secretary of Defense, the Aerospace Audio Visual Service, and the Signal Corps. Particular thanks are due to Lt. Colonel Robert A. Webb, USAF, who was the liaison officer on the project.

Acknowledgment is also made herewith for permission to quote from the following books: *Decision in Germany* by Lucius Clay, Copyright 1950 by Lucius Clay, and used by permission of Doubleday & Company, Inc.; and *Over the Hump* by William H. Tunner, Copyright © 1964 by William H. Tunner and Booton Herndon, published by Duell, Sloan & Pearce, Inc.

Index